·Bartholomew·

WALK OBAN,
MULL AND LOCHABER

by Richard Hallewell

Illustrations by Rebecca Johnstone

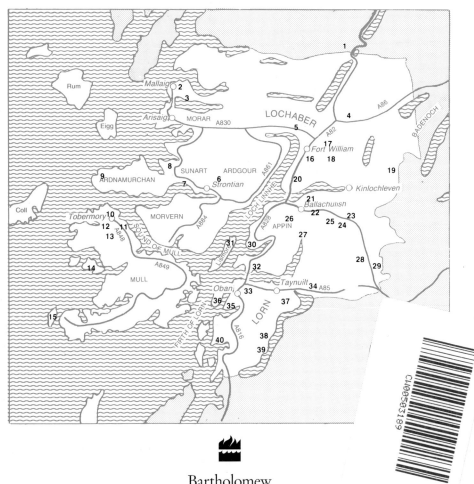

Bartholomew

An Imprint of HarperCollins*Publishers*

A Bartholomew Walk Guide
Published by Bartholomew
An Imprint of HarperCollins*Publishers*
77-85 Fulham Palace Road
London W6 8JB

First published 1988
Revised 1993
Reprinted 1994
Reprinted with amendments 1996
Reprinted 1997

Printed in Hong Kong

ISBN 0 7028 3260 X

88/2/52

KJ 9484

About this book

This is a book of walks, each of which can be completed within one day. They pass through every type of scenery to be found in the area - mountain, coastal and moorland - and vary in difficulty from gentle strolls to strenuous hill climbs. Each route is graded according to its level of difficulty, and wherever specialist hill-walking equipment is required this is specified. There is a description of each route, including information on the character and condition of the paths, and with a brief description of the major points of interest along the way. In addition there is a sketch map of the route to aid navigation. Car parks, where available, are indicated on the route maps. The availability of public conveniences and public transport on particular routes is listed on the contents page, and at the head of each route. The suitability or otherwise of the route for dogs is also indicated on the contents page. The location of each route within the area is shown on the area map inside the cover of the book, and a brief description of how to reach the walk from the nearest town is provided at the start of each walk. In addition, National Grid References are provided on the maps. The use of a detailed map, in addition to this book, is advised on all grade A walks.

The following introduction provides a brief summary of the geology, history and natural history of the area; listing (within the limitations of space) the people of consequence who have been associated with the area, and indicating the places where incidents of historical importance occurred. Hopefully, an appreciation of these links with the past will add to the interest of the walks.

Before setting out, all walkers are asked to read through the section of Advice to Walkers at the end of the introduction. In the long term it never pays to become lax in taking safety precautions.

This is by no means an exhaustive list of the excellent walks throughout this area, but it provides a core of varied, accepted routes. I hope you will find it an interesting selection.

Key

●●●	Route	⧸⧸ ⧸⧸	Marshland
═══	Metalled Road	⋯⋯	Moorland
┼┼┼┼┼	Railway	▲ ▲	Coniferous Woodland
Ⓟ	Parking	◆ ◆	Broad-leaved Woodland
i	Information Centre	50ₘ	Contour: shaded area
⅃	Viewpoint		is above height indicated

INTRODUCTION

The Area

(Numbers in italics refer to individual routes)

This area is famous for its climbing and hill walking, and is a favourite destination for many visitors to Scotland, but, until the end of the 18th century, it was considered far too lawless, and the country too rough, for general travellers. The earliest visitors were inspired by the new craze of Romanticism, which considered the natural world - and the Highlands were undeniably 'natural', as well as conveniently close - to be the paradigm of beauty. Romanticism was largely triggered by the works of James 'Ossian' Macpherson; the bogus 'translations' of 'Gaelic epics' which brought their author great fortune and fame throughout Europe, and first applied that patina of sentimentalism to the Highlands which remains both a curse and a blessing to this day.

Ironically, these early travellers - Boswell and Johnson, the Wordsworths, Mendelssohn and others - were only able to tour the Highlands because of the construction of military roads throughout the area; the purpose of which was to help in the dismantling of the society which had produced the originals of the works they so admired.

Despite these roads travel was still extremely spartan, and travellers remained scarce until the opening of the railways in the 19th century, and the expansion of the terminus towns of Fort William and Oban. In more recent years the improvement of the road system has opened up the area to large numbers of visitors; while those who wish to enter the area on foot can do so along the West Highland Way: Scotland's first long distance footpath, opened in 1980.

The area which has drawn these visitors down the years contains some of the grandest scenery in Britain, including many features which have become clichés of the Highland landscape, so often have they appeared on postcards, shortbread tins and every conceivable tourist gewgaw - Ben Nevis, Glen Coe, Castle Stalker, Oban Bay. In general it is a landscape of harsh character; high, steep, rocky hills; intersected by narrow glens and long, thin, deep freshwater lochs; the coastline jagged and deeply indented by long sea-lochs: arms of the green Atlantic which reach far into the interior of the land.

The rocks which form this extravagant landscape are largely igneous or metamorphic: granite and basalt, formed by volcanic activity millions of years ago, and carved to their present shape by the glaciers of the ice age.

The ice had a profound effect upon the nature of the area. The high plateaux of volcanic rocks were gradually eroded by successive coverings of ice; any weak sections of the rock being ground out of the matrix, forming glens and corries.

The main gathering point for the ice in the west Highlands was on the eastern edge of this area, on what is now Rannoch Moor *(19)*: a wide undulating basin of damp moorland, still littered with the debris deposited when the ice melted, some 8000 years ago; pitted with shallow lochs of irregular shape, and scarred by the open peat banks of the burns which meander across the open moorland.

The ice which collected on Rannoch was dispersed in all directions in the form of glaciers, grinding slowly down the glens which radiate from the moor like the spokes of a wheel: Loch Rannoch, Loch Ericht, Loch Ossian *(19)*, Loch Treig, Glen Nevis *(18)*, Loch Leven *(23)*, Glen Coe *(21-25)*, Glen Etive *(24,27)* and Glen Orchy *(28,29)*. During the period of glaciation these glens were gradually ground into the broad, U-shaped valleys with steep, rocky sides which are so typical of a glaciated landscape. The rocks and gravel removed by the ice were carried by the glaciers until they melted; being deposited either as erratics (individual rocks, scattered across the landscape) or as the gravel beds which now fill the floors of the glens. It was this process which made the Highlands so harsh a landscape.

One specific side effect of the ice was the creation of the 'parallel roads'. These are long, even terraces visible on the sides of some of the glens, and were formed as the shorelines of lochs dammed by the glaciers. This feature is particularly conspicuous in Glen Roy *(4)*.

Following the retreat of the ice and the removal of the great burden of its weight the land seems to have risen, creating the raised beaches which are such a feature of the Scottish coast, and which are particularly evident in Argyll *(14,30,31,35,36)*, where they are often backed by the sea-worn cliffs which once lined the shore. This feature is missing from the upper reaches of the long sea-lochs, which were usually masked by ice until a later period than the rest of the coast.

These lochs have always been a serious obstacle to travel through the area, and still often necessitate long detours for the coastal roads, but they do perform the function of bringing the Gulf Stream - a comparatively warm current of water, flowing north from the equator - into the heart of the hills, thus mollifying the winter cold. Even palm trees can occasionally be seen growing in sheltered spots along the coast.

The presence of the Atlantic also has an effect on the level of precipitation throughout the area; a subject of great interest to walkers. The prevailing westerlies carry a great deal of moisture, which has been picked up while crossing the ocean. The air rises as it crosses the high land and deposits great quantities of rain over the hills. It would be pointless to deny that parts of the area are very wet indeed, but others are comparatively dry. The dampest area in Britain lies in a narrow strip; starting around Glen Orchy *(28,29)* and extending, slightly west of north, through Rannoch *(19)*, Glen Coe *(21-25)* and Ben Nevis *(17)* and on to Knapdale. This area receives, on average, over three times the annual precipitation of eastern England. However, the land to the west of the hills, on the islands and the low lying coastal areas, is only half as damp as the inland strip. When the wind is in the east (ie, approaching across the continent) the weather is generally colder and dryer.

One problem caused by this comparatively high rainfall is that it tends to make the ground very wet, and there is insufficient sunshine (particularly on north facing-slopes) to dry out the soil by evaporation. As a result, many walks remain damp throughout the year.

This dampness has been exacerbated by the felling of the area's forests.

Following the retreat of the ice the Highlands were gradually colonised by trees: predominantly birch and Scots pine inland and on the poorer soils and north facing slopes, and oak on the south facing slopes of the western glens and lochs. Very little of these once vast forests now remains - generations of clearing through fire (intentional or accidental) and felling for agriculture, fuel or building have largely denuded the hills. Small pockets remain however; the more valued for their contraction and rarity - a patch of pine forest around the head of Loch Tulla on the edge of Rannoch Moor *(28)*, and the soft, mossy oakwoods of Loch Awe *(37,38)*, Loch Creran, Loch Sunart *(6,7)* and South Morar.

Where this forest has been cleared the almost universal cover is of grass or heather moorland. In addition, in recent years, large areas have been given over to plantations of commercial conifers *(16,19 20,21,26,28,32,39)*. Whatever the commercial, political and employment value of these plantations, they have never seriously been defended on aesthetic grounds.

The major peaks in the area are Ben More (3169ft/966m) on Mull, Ben Cruachan (3693ft/1126m) *(34)* by Loch Awe and Ben Nevis (4408ft/1344m) *(17)* - the highest mountain in Britain - to the east of Fort William. In addition, there are virtually continuous ranges throughout the area; notably the hills of Mamore Forest (this term can be misleading; it refers to deer forests, which rarely have any trees at all) to the south of Ben Nevis, the peaks around Beinn Dòrain *(29)* to the east of Glen Orchy, and the great knot of hills to the west of Rannoch Moor, surrounding Glen Etive, Glen Coe and upper Glen Creran *(21-27)*.

The largest of the sea-lochs is Loch Linnhe, which was ground from the broken rocks around the Great Glen fault by the glaciers. It leads 30 miles from the southern tip of the Morvern peninsula to Fort William (at the southern end of the Caledonian Canal *(5)*, which then continues along the glen for a further 60 miles to Inverness, on the Moray Firth), cuts sharply to the west and continues another 10 miles as Loch Eil. This loch, and the Great Glen to the north, effectively separate the accessible south-west Highlands from the bleaker and more remote north-west.

Three other major lochs cut east from Linnhe: Loch Etive *(27)*, Loch Creran and Loch Leven. To the west the Sound of Mull cuts between Morvern and the island of Mull. The main lochs to the north of Morvern are Loch Sunart *(6,7)*, the Sound of Arisaig, Loch Nevis *(3)* and Loch Huorn.

The area also contains a number of large inland lochs; generally, like the sea-lochs, long and thin. The largest is Loch Awe *(39)* (over 20 miles long); set amongst the low hills at the southern end of this area, with its northern end scattered with small, wooded islands. The deepest in the area (and possibly in Scotland) is Loch Morar *(3)*, south of Mallaig. Morar is over 1000ft deep near its eastern end, although its surface level is only about 50ft above sea-level. Other major natural lochs include Loch Arkaig and Loch Shiel north-west of the Great Glen; Loch Oich and Loch Lochy in the glen itself; Loch Laggan in Badenoch, in the north-east; Loch Ossian *(19)* to the north of Rannoch Moor; and Loch Laidon on the moor itself. In addition, there are a number of lochs which have been created or enlarged for hydro-electric power; notably Lochs Quoich, Cluanie, Garry, and Treig, and the Blackwater Reservoir.

Because of the abrupt rise of the hills from the sea, and the propinquity of the east-west watershed to the coast, there are no long rivers in the area. Nonetheless, the high rainfall over the hills ensures that they are full, and the steepness of the terrain makes them swift-flowing; a characteristic which impeded early travel through the area.

Such descriptions might suggest an unrelieved landscape of dark mountains shrouded in mist, with white torrents rushing down their flanks into murky lochs; rather as the Highlands were depicted in early Victorian prints. This is certainly one face of the area, but not the only one: the summers are often punctuated by long periods of very bright, very warm weather, heightened by the reflective power of the ubiquitous lochs and sea-lochs. Such periods are characterised by a very pure light, a feature which attracted many late-19th and early-20th century painters (D Y Cameron, MacTaggart, and the colourists Caddell, Peploe and Fergusson) to the west coast, and particularly to Morar *(2,3)*, Moidart *(8)*, Ardnamurchan *(9)*, Mull and Iona *(15)*, where, on sunny days, the white sands show turquoise through the clear, green waters.

The general cover of the land is of moorland (utilised as rough grazing for sheep) and forestry, but in places this gives way to patches of fertile land. These occur along the raised beaches (where there are terraces of soil enriched by the past cover of sea weed and shell-sand), and on the machair behind the current beaches. Other green areas exist on the volcanic and sedimentary rocks, such as the broad basalt terraces of Mull *(12,13)* and the limestone of Lismore *(31)*. The steep and rocky nature of the land permits only small patches of arable farming, and this more fertile land is generally used for cattle-grazing.

Crofting is still common in parts of this area; particularly in the north and west. Crofts are generally composed of a small area of relatively fertile land (usually along the coast) for crops; backed by a rough hill for grazing animals. In the past crofting was the major source of employment for the people of the area; its limited rewards being augmented by seasonal participation in the fishing industry. In the present day many crofters are still involved in fishing, while others have taken to fish-farming (the large rafts containing the fish can be seen anchored in many bays along the coast) or tourism.

Much of the land is still owned by large estates, and the high moors are maintained for deer-stalking and grouse shooting.

Modern, large scale industry has not had a particularly rosy history in the Highlands, but there are still aluminium works at Kinlochleven *(23)* and Fort William, and some light industry around the two main towns: Oban and Fort William.

The population is not large, and it has always tended to be scattered in small settlements. During the last two hundred years there has been considerable centralisation, and the main towns have slowly grown, but it is still largely a rural population. The two main centres apart, there are no towns of any size, and services are often far apart along the roads, so it is important to plan well ahead before driving to the remoter corners.

Oban is principally a tourist town, but it also has a hard commercial edge to it. It is the ferry terminus for Colonsay, Mull, Coll, Tiree and the Outer Isles; a fishing harbour; a market town and a sevice centre for a wide area of the south-west Highlands.

Fort William is a damper and less attractive spot, tucked away at the head of Loch Linnhe and rather overshadowed by Ben Nevis and the surrounding peaks. The town is more industrial than Oban, but it fills a similar role as service centre to the surrounding glens. In addition, it is undoubtedly the hill-walkers and back-packers capital of Scotland, and has a number of shops catering for the requirements of the sport.

The other main settlements in the area are Mallaig *(2)*: a busy fishing port on the Sound of Sleat; Ballachulish *(26)* on the south side of Loch Leven; and Tobermory *(10,11)* which, although small, is the only settlement of any size on Mull, and thus carries most of the services.

These towns are spread throughout some of the finest walking country in Scotland. This book contains a range of routes, covering, in as far as it is possible, every type of terrain and every corner of the area. Naturally, only a few of the many can be included.

The walking in Lorn, at the southern end of the area *(33-40)*, tends to be low-level, through the grassy hills and mixed farmland of the area; or coastal, along the raised beaches. In addition, there are a number of routes in the area through conifer plantations and the old oakwoods along Loch Awe. Offshore are the pleasant islands of Kerrera *(36)*, Seil, Luing and others. These three mentioned can all be reached by ferry, and all provide pleasant walking.

At the north end of Loch Awe is Ben Cruachan *(34)*, and beyond are the moors and high hills of Glen Orchy *(28,29)* and Rannoch. This is an area best suited to climbing and longer hill walks. The same is also true of the area of hills to the west, around Loch Etive, Glen Etive and Glen Coe *(21-25,27)* and the hills of Benderloch *(32)* and Appin beyond them, but in this area there is also pleasant coastal walking *(30)*, and access to the green island of Lismore *(31)*.

Appin's northern boundary is Loch Leven, beyond which are the hills of Lochaber, east of Fort William *(16,18,20)*, including Ben Nevis *(17)*. These descend to the east towards the bogs of Rannoch Moor *(19)*.

Across the Firth of Lorn from Oban is Mull; the second largest of the Inner Hebrides after Skye. There is extensive walking amongst its high, grassy hills, along its coast *(10-13)*, and on the off-lying islands *(14,15)*.

The land north of Mull and the west of the Great Glen - Morvern, Ardnamurchan *(9)*, Ardgour, Sunart *(6,7)*, Moidart *(8)*, Morar *(2,3)* and Knoydart is scarcely touched on in this book. This does not mean that the area is unsuitable for walking, simply that the routes tend to be so long, and often so time-consuming to reach, that they fall without the remit of this guide. Similarly, the Small Isles (Rum, Eigg, Canna and Muck), Coll, Tiree and Colonsay are well worth visiting, and are omitted only because of the time required to reach them.

Longer tracks throughout the area are covered in other publications. The West Highland Publications series covers much of the mainland, and gives notes of the historical background of many of the possible longer routes. In addition, there are two booklets published on walks in Mull. These publications are all available locally.

History

Those early travellers, inspired by the Romantic illusions of Macpherson; their travels given the added piquancy of danger by the recent warlike past of the Highlanders, found a very different country to that which they had left behind them; from which it could be differentiated in both language and customs, and in the material poverty of its inhabitants. Most of them, however, being ignorant of the Gaelic language and of the history and manners of the place, and finding the people generally pacific and friendly, seem to have concluded that people are not essentially different the world over, and were happy enough to return to the affluent lands to the south; impressed more by the grandeur of the Highlands than by its inhabitants.

However, the history of the Highlands has, for long spells, been divorced from that of the rest of Britain; and, if it is composed of those same elements of humanity - pride, valour, spite, generosity - as any other history, it has as least, for most people, the freshness of the unknown, and the romance of its splendid, scenic backdrop.

It has, besides, the appeal of a receding fragrance. The land is almost empty of physical reminders of the past ages; a few old castles remain, but little else to suggest the unique and thriving society which once existed here. The Gaelic culture, as all Celtic cultures, has left few visible remains. There are no old towns or palaces where one can guess the nature of past builders; the only monuments the Gaels built were in words: their poems, in which, assuming a knowledge amongst their listeners of a lifestyle and a set of attitudes which had not significantly changed even in the length of folk memory, the bards concentrated upon the perfection of complex formal schemes of rhyme, rhythm and alliteration: those very qualities which cannot successfully be translated. Nonethless, a handful of poets who worked near the close of Highland society, often inspired by a knowledge of the work of English and classical poets, and who had travelled sufficiently outside the Highlands to observe their culture more objectively, did produce work which can help the layman appreciate their time and place, and the unique society which had, by a trick of history, developed here.

Following the ice age, and contemporary with the spread of the great forests which eventually covered most of the country, the first people arrived in Scotland from the continent. This initial, and tentative, influx of stone-age hunters was followed, over the next nine millennia, by a succession of waves of immigrants; exiles or conquerors from the warmer, more civilized and advanced lands in southern Europe and the Middle East, who each, in turn, achieved ascendancy over the inhabitants of Scotland by the agency of superior weaponry, discipline or attitude, and who then slowly blended with their predecessors into a hybrid race, the descendants of which are the modern Scots. There is no reason to suppose that the current inhabitants do not include, in some measure, the genes of the earliest cave-dwellers of these islands.

In the late bronze-age, in the millenium before Christ, the crannog-builders were busy throughout Scotland, building low islands in shallow lochs as foundations for their round wooden huts *(39)*. Loch Awe has a great many of these little islands and must once have been busy with the canoes of their builders.

These people were the earliest Celtic inhabitants of Scotland, and they were followed, around 600BC, by invaders from a more warlike branch of the same people, who had, besides, mastered the art of working iron.

The Celts were a widely-spread people who inhabited most of central Europe. After they had been conquered by the Romans on the European mainland their culture - evanescent and ill-sustained as always - quickly vanished, eventually surviving only in those areas on the periphery of Europe - Brittany, Cornwall, Wales, Scotland and Ireland - where the poverty of the land discouraged the Romans from widespread colonisation, and sufficiently precluded agriculture to make the warrior life a profitable alternative. In this area this life style was followed until the end of the 18th century.

The iron-age Celts built dry-stone forts, the most substantial of which were the brochs. These most impressive structures are largely confined to the far north of Scotland, but there are some examples in this area; on Tiree and Mull and at Tirefour on Lismore *(31)*. The brochs take the form of round funnels, 20-40ft high, attenuating towards the top, with thick walls and one low doorway. As with all Highland defensive buildings, the brochs, intentionally or otherwise, give the illusion of great size while actually being very small - the internal floor of a broch was only 30-40ft in diameter.

The height of the broch-builders' industry was a little after the birth of Christ, after which the structures seem to have become obsolete and were soon abandoned; unlike the crannogs, some of which were still in use as defensive sites as late as the 16th century.

Around the time of the broch-builders, Ireland was divided into a number of petty kingdoms; ruled by such as the semi-mythical King Conchobor of Ulster and Queen Medb of Connaught, two of the central figures in the Ulster cycle of tales concerning Cúchulainn and the warriors of the Red Branch. These tales were handed down orally for many centuries before being written down by monks in the 12th century, and continued to be widely told thereafter.

The importance of these tales lies in the sense of timeless continuity which they must have instilled in their hearers. The central story of the cycle, for instance, is the Tain Bo Cuailnge; the story of a great cattle raid; wound around, to be sure, with implausible heroics and the interference of the gods, but at heart a clan war involving characters, battles and situations which were entirely recognisable and contemporary to the Highlanders as late as the 18th century. In addition, the stories delineated a code of behaviour, centred on obligations and honour, and the recognition of a brave enemy, which, if not universally honoured, was at least recognised as an ideal. Thus, when the 17th century bard of Keppoch, Iain Lom, having heard that the Campbell chief, the Duke of Argyll, had put a price on his head for the scurrility of his invective against the clan, travelled south to collect the reward in person, the bravery of the act was recognised by Argyll, who rewarded the poet with a week's entertainment in Inverary.

The only direct connection between the Ulster Cycle and this area is Glen Etive, where the beautiful Derdriu and her lover Noisiu are traditionally believed to have fled when pursued by King Conchobor, to whom Derdriu was betrothed.

In later years such a flight would simply have been geographical, from one branch of the Gaels to another; but at that time it was also cultural, since the north of Scotland was inhabited by the Picts; a hybrid race who spoke a language which is thought to have been related to Welsh and Breton, although not a sentence of it has survived.

In the early centuries AD there seems to have been a slow colonisation of Argyll (Erraghidheal - *'the Coastland of the Gaels'*) by the Gaels of Ireland (known to the Romans as the Scotti); an immigration which is perhaps at the root of the tale of Derdriu.

This colonisation was made official when Fergus Mór Mac Eirc, the king of Dalriada in Ireland, moved to Argyll in AD 500. Over the next 350 years his descendents extended their influence over most of mainland Scotland. The current royal family are descended from these early Scottish kings.

The kingdom of Dalriada was divided, by the late 7th century, into four groups, who took their names from the royal personage from whom their ruling line was descended: Cenél nGabrain in Kintyre, Arran and Jura; Cenél nOengusa in Islay; Cenel Comgaill in Cowal; and the Cenel Loairn - who gave their name to the area of Lorn - from a little below the southern edge of the area covered in this book, north to Ardnamurchan. The Cenel Loairn's main centres were at Dunadd, near Crinan, and Dunollie near Oban. The High-Kingship over Dalriada was passed between the various royal houses: a system known as 'tanistry'.

This remembrance of ancestors in place and family names was a characteristic of the Gaels, who prided themselves on a long and noble ancestry. The Campbells, for instance, traced the lineage of their chiefs back to Diarmaid, the semi-mythical companion of Finn MacCumhaill: a figure who, with his warrior band, the Fíann, featured in many oral tales and poems. The Irish immigrants imported the stories, and changed the scene of the action to the Highlands; hence place names such as 'Sgorr nam Fiannaidh', in Glencoe. It was these folk tales which James Macpherson, at the end of the 18th century, 'translated' as examples of the great Highland epics, to the wonder of Europe.

There was continual warfare between the new kingdom of Dalriada and the native Picts, and in the 8th century the numerical superiority of the Picts seemed likely to destroy the Scots in Argyll, and yet, within 100 years Kenneth McAlpin of Dalriada was the ruler of both kingdoms, and Pictish culture had begun its swift decline.

The Scots' ability to survive was partly due to their ability to call on reinforcements from Ireland, and partly to the moral authority which they held through their guardianship of Iona, the cradle of Scottish Christianity.

The man responsible for Iona's importance was Columba, an Irish prince who founded a community on the island in 563. There were other important missionaries in the area at the time - notably Moluag, on Lismore - but it was Columba who made the most impact, and who is remembered today.

In 565 he journeyed up the Great Glen to meet the Pictish king, Brude, at Inverness. His conversion of the king, and the permission he received to spread the Gaelic church - and, thus, the Gaelic culture - throughout Pictland, signalled the start of the erosion of Pictish culture.

The job was completed by the vikings, who began a series of raids on the British Isles around the end of the 8th century.

The weapon which enabled the vikings to make the impact they did was the longship. The Scots and the Picts were able seamen - Dalriada was largely a kingdom of islands, and its subjects were required to supply galleys as well as men at arms - but their vessels lacked the sea-going capacity of the longships. In addition, the country was only sparsely populated, and the people were scattered in small communities, so little help could be expected for victims of an attack. In sum, the viking raids were impossible to anticipate, repulse or revenge.

Iona, Lismore and other island sites which held church, and thus cultural, treasures were now open to attacks at any time from the pagan invaders, who did not waste their opportunity.

The Scots and the Picts were driven inland by this mutual foe, and gradually became unified under the Gaelic language, church, culture and, in 843, king.

The Norse were initially content to raid. However, a population explosion in western Norway encouraged many people to look for homes in the lands to the west. Norse colonisation began around 800, and gradually spread throughout the isles. In 1098 a treaty between King Magnus Bareleg of Norway and King Edgar of Scotland confirmed that the western isles, the Isle of Man and Kintyre were under Norwegian sovereignty.

The effect of this intrusion was to create a buffer state between the Scottish and Irish Gaels, which led to their gradual divergence. Some contact continued; particularly, in later centuries, between the Scottish and Irish branches of Clan Donald, and through the continual use of 'galloglasses', the Scottish Gaelic/Norse mercenaries, in Irish wars, but this never amounted to the former political unity.

Although ostensibly under Norwegian rule, the western islands were too distant from Scandinavia to be effectively governed, and the islanders naturally began to become involved in more local alliances and disputes. Nonetheless, the Norwegians held the land until the mid-13th century, when King Haakon was defeated at Largs by Alexander III of Scotland, and died in Orkney soon afterwards. In 1266 the Treaty of Perth was signed, and the western isles were sold to the Scottish king.

By this time the line of Gaelic/Celtic kings had been superseded by the House of Canmore, which was based upon an Anglo-Norman system and aristocracy, and which maintained close links with the English court. In addition, the religious capital had been transported eastwards; from Iona to Dunkeld, and thence to St Andrews. The majority of the country were still Gaelic speakers, and the Highland aristocracy still played a central role in Scottish politics, but this influence gradually declined until, under the Stewart monarchs, the Highlanders began increasingly to be seen as an alien, potentially dangerous force, rather than as an integral part of the kingdom.

When the line of Canmore ended, with the death of Alexander III in 1286, Scotland was thrown into the turmoil of the Wars of Independence, as first William Wallace and then Robert the Bruce strove to keep Scotland free of English rule.

Allegiance to the Anglo-Norman Scottish aristocracy was not assured in the west, and there were so many rival claimants to the throne that even those inclined towards independence could not be relied upon for support. The principal clan in the area at the time were the MacDougalls, a Gaelic/Norse family who held strong castles at Dunstaffnage and Dunollie and extensive lands in Lorn and the Islands. The MacDougalls were related by marriage to the Comyns, who were rival claimants with Bruce for the throne, and were also in contact with King Edward I of England; thus, they were opposed to Bruce. In 1308 they ambushed him at the narrow Pass of Brander, in the shadow of Ben Cruachan. Bruce anticipated the attack and outmanoeuvred his assailants, and, when the war was over and he had time to review his friends and enemies, he split most of the MacDougall lands between those families who had proved more supportive - principally the early representatives of the great Campbell and MacDonald dynasties.

In the following centuries lowland and Highland Scotland developed separately. Both societies were hamstrung by weak leadership, dissension and poverty, but the Lowlands can be seen to have been progressing, if tardily, in the wake of the rest of northern Europe; through feudalism to the Renaissance and the Reformation. These movements had little impact in the Highlands, and the only partial success of the Reformation left a stump of Catholicism in the north and west which was exploited during the following centuries.

The system followed in the Highlands was broadly that introduced by the Irish into Dalriada, where groups were bound by a real or imagined common ancestry. It was a military society, and a chief would measure his wealth in the number of men which he could bring to a battle field. Such emphasis on strength was essential in a land where legal powers and documentation of ownership counted for little. For example, the MacDonalds of Keppoch were a recognised branch of the clan, yet the lands they occupied (around Glen Spean and Glen Roy) legally belonged to the Mackintoshes.

The coinage of the clans was cattle, which provided the only major source of funds to an area which was otherwise largely self-supporting. The export of cattle to the south had been practiced from early times, but it reached its peak in the 18th and 19th centuries, when many thousands of cattle were driven to the great trysts, or cattle markets, at Falkirk and Crieff. Many of the 'drove-roads' along which the cattle were driven criss-cross this area; including the track across Kerrera *(36)*, the Devil's Staircase,

north from Glen Coe *(23)*, and the track from Inveroran to Tyndrum *(28,29)*. Alongside this legal and profitable trade there flourished an equally profitable but quite illegal rash of cattle-raiding; which was both the root, and the means of conducting, much of the clan warfare.

At various times different clans would establish an ascendancy over their neighbours, draw support, swell in importance and then, having earned the jealousy and hatred of those at whose expense they had expanded, stumble and decline.

The first powerful clan had been the MacDougalls; who had lost much of their land by opposing Bruce. The subsequent power vacuum was largely filled by the descendants of Angus Òg of Islay (chief of the MacDonalds), who had received the island of Mull in payment for supporting Bruce, and had adopted the title of 'Lord of the Isles'. His son, by adroit politics and careful marriage, extended the rule of the MacDonalds over most of the mainland area of this book, plus Kintyre and Knapdale to the south and most of the major islands off the west coast, with the exception of Skye.

The existence of this huge province, virtually an independant kingdom, established, for a while, centralised and internal rule in Gaelic Scotland; and encouraged a brief flourishing of Gaelic culture and learning.

Inevitably, however, the MacDonalds over extended themselves; trying to add the unwilling Earldom of Ross (including Skye) to their wide possessions, and entering into treasonable negotiations with Edward IV of England and the Earl of Douglas in 1462; planning the eviction of the Stewarts and the division of Scotland between themselves.

From this point onwards the powers of the Lords of the Isles waned, and their lands were divided amongst clans more loyal to the crown; notably the Campbells.

The next three hundred years of the area's history is a catalogue of the murders, battles and deceits which marked the gradual expansion of this great clan at the expense of its neighbours to the north: the MacDougalls around Oban; the Stewarts of Appin (with their much-photographed stronghold of Castle Stalker on a small island in the mud flats of Loch Laich); the Camerons in the glens around the head of Loch Linnhe; the MacLeans in Mull, Morvern and Ardgour; and the various branches of the MacDonalds: Clanranald in the Small Isles, Moidart and Ardnamurchan; the MacDonells of Glengarry west of the Great Glen; and the two smaller branches of Keppoch and Glen Coe.

Clan warfare in this period was often presented as being part of the broader, religious disputes which caused strife throughout Europe from the Reformation onwards, but it was usually firmly rooted in Highland politics. It is notable that, whatever the dispute, the Campbells and their northern neighbours would conspire to fight on opposite sides; the MacDonalds hoping for that single victory which would reverse their decline and restore their previous influence, and the smaller clans simply wishing to be free of the incessant plotting and manipulation by which the Campbells slowly ate into their posessions.

There were reversals of course; the most notable of which was the brief Highland campaign of the Marquess of Montrose in 1644-45.

The excuse was the war between the Royalists and the Covenanters, but the alignments were the same as ever; with the Duke of Argyll in command of the forces of the Covenant, and Montrose, with his Catholic Irishmen and Highlanders, fighting for King Charles I.

Montrose came to the Highlands with nothing but two companions and the King's commission as Lieutenant-General, but he raised an army and crushed all opposition in a swift, brilliant campaign. At the close of 1644 he harried the Campbell heartland of Argyll, with the joyous support of the MacDonalds. His small army then travelled north, along the Great Glen. While in the glen Montrose received word that there were two armies in the field against him; closing in from the north and the south. Exhibiting his ability to inspire an army to attempt the unexpected, and attempt it with success, Montrose doubled back, cut through the snow-filled passes above Glen Roy *(4)* and around the northern edge of Ben Nevis - a two day march, swift enough to precede any intelligence of his approach - to confront the Duke of Argyll's army at Inverlochy, near the head of Loch Linnhe. Taken completely by surprise, the army of Campbells and Lowlanders was routed, and around 1500 were killed.

Montrose continued on his victorious road, but with every mile he marched towards his southern objectives his Highland army, interested only in the discomfiture of their neighbours, evaporated. The Royalist army was surprised and routed at Philiphaugh, near Selkirk, and Montrose fled; only to be captured and hanged when leading another campaign in the northern Highlands.

The bard Iain Lom was present at Inverlochy, and wrote his most quoted poem in celebration; describing with evident relish a battlefield '...manured, not by the dung of sheep or goats, but by the congealed blood of Campbells'. Within five years the poet had composed elegies for both Montrose and the giant Alasdair MacColla, who had led the MacDonalds in the fray.

In the 18th century another famous MacDonald poet, Alasdair Mac Mhaighstir Alasdair, lived in this area. He was born around 1700, near the southern tip of Loch Shiel; the son of an Episcopalian minister and descended from the chiefs of Clanranald. Like Iain Lom before him he took an interest and a part in the politics of the time, but he was a man of a different stamp: similarly proud and touchy, but exuberant and passionate where Iain Lom had been sly and hard.

Alasdair, though employed as a schoolmaster in the Presbyterian school in Ardnamurchan, strongly supported the Catholic Jacobites, and joined the Stewart army in 1745 as a captain; but despite this, and his great love of the Highlands and of the Gaelic language, he was no bigot, and recognised, perhaps, the trend in events. In 1741 he produced the first Gaelic-English dictionary, with the express intention of encouraging the Highlanders to become bilingual.

In the period preceding the arrival of Charles Stewart, Alasdair made every attempt to drum up enthusiasm for the cause, but popular support for the Stewarts was not as strong as is often believed. The political position of the Highlands had changed in the hundred years since Montrose's victory at Inverlochy. The Union of Scotland and England in 1707 had changed the Highlanders from a powerful majority to a dangerous minority - an obvious source of support for the deposed line of the Stewarts - and there was every reason to believe that King William - naturally fearful of any popular uprising - was simply waiting for an excuse to neutralise the danger.

The lengths to which Government was prepared to go to keep the peace in the region had been shown by the Massacre of Glen Coe in 1692, in which the MacIan (chief of the MacDonalds of Glen Coe) and 40 or so of his clan were killed by two battalions of the Duke of Argyll's regiment, whom they had been entertaining in the glen for some days. The excuse for the act was that the MacIan had failed to sign an oath of allegiance to William - whom all the clans were required to officially recognise - by a set date. He had not been the only chief slow to come forward, however, and it was clear that an example was being set. Similarly, there was

harsh retribution meted out to the ring-leaders after the rising in 1715. Many did not care to find out what the response to further trouble might be.

Nonetheless, central authority was resented, and the ties of loyalty - which were the mainstay of the clan system - were still strong. In addition, many of the clans had little to lose: including the Macleans, who had lost virtually everything (including Duart Castle) to the Campbells, the MacGregors of Rannoch and Glen Strae, who were prohibited even from using their name under pain of death, the Camerons, the Stewarts of Appin and, of course, the MacDonalds. Thus, the supporters who ralleyed to Charles Stewart after he had landed at Loch nan Uamh, in Moidart, and raised his standard at Glenfinnan, at the head of Loch Shiel (the place is now marked by a monument), were taking a desperate gamble.

The Prince passed through Moidart again, in 1746; this time dodging his pursuers while waiting for the boat which would take him to the continent, following the conclusion of the rising after the rout at Culloden.

In the immediate aftermath of the battle the Hanoverian army, led by the Duke of Cumberland, acted with some brutality; executing prisoners out of hand and hunting the vanquished forces through the hills. Some escaped, with the Prince, to Europe; others, such as Simon Fraser, Lord Lovat, were less lucky. Fraser was captured when he was found hiding in a tree stump on an island in Loch Morar.

In addition, many of the clansmen were imprisoned or transported; the lands of the Jacobite chiefs were forfeited to the crown, and the Disarming and Disclothing Acts (the latter proscribing the bagpipes and the kilt) were passed.

Such excessive measures were scarcely necessary, but the crown had been genuinely frightened by the initial success of the rising, and there was a natural urge not to leave the job half completed.

Within a very short time the policy could be seen to have succeeded. The Hanoverian chiefs, and those Jacobite chiefs who had been pardoned, were busy raising regiments for the British army. The outstanding service of these regiments created so favourable an impression with both the authorities and southern public opinion that the Highlanders were soon entirely forgiven. Before the end of the century the bans were lifted and the forfeited estates returned to their owners.

Much had changed however; not least the nature of the bonds between the chiefs and their clansmen. Highland noblemen, now requiring sufficient money to fund the life of a gentleman and the expensive tastes of Georgian society, raised rents or sought alternative and more renumerative uses for the land.

Not all chiefs were bad in this respect, but each, in turn, was forced to succumb to the painful necessities of cramming centuries of progress into a few years, and to admitting that there were simply too many people (the population was rising steadily at the time) for the land to support.

Some local industries were started, such as the iron furnace at Bonawe, and there was also slate quarrying at Ballachulish, and lead mining at Tyndrum and Strontian; while along the coast an expansion of the fishing industry was encouraged. Such measures, however, could never hope to soak up all of the population, which was gradually being removed from the hills - often forcibly - to make way for sheep.

Many of the common people elected, or were encouraged, to leave the Highlands completely; either travelling south to work in the new factories of the Industrial Revolution, or leaving the country altogether and emigrating to the new promise of the expanding Empire, every corner of which is populated by the descendants of the Highlanders.

Place Names

The distribution of place names in a specific language provides an indication to the areas inhabited by the people who spoke that language. This is particularly useful in a country such as Scotland, where, during the dark ages, there were several co-existing groups using different languages - Welsh-speaking Britons in the south-west; English-speaking Angles in the south-east; Picts in the north; Gaelic-speaking Scots in the west; and vikings in the islands - and where there are comparatively few concrete remains to indicate the homelands of the various cultures.

This area was inhabited by the Picts until 200-300 AD, when the first Scots began to arrive. The fact that there are no remaining Pictish place names indicates either that the Pictish population was very small in the west, or that the colonisation was strongly resisted; otherwise the Scots would have adopted the existing Pictish place names.

On the islands and along the coast there are some Scandinavian place names; reflecting the spread of the vikings. Much the most common elememt is 'dale', meaning a valley.

Virtually all of the remaining place names in this area are of Gaelic origin. A list of the commonest Gaelic elements is given below, but don't be surprised if the map spelling differs from that shown: this is due partly to the anglicisation of the words and partly to Gaelic grammar, which causes nouns and adjectives to alter, depending on their use in the sentence. One final tip. In Gaelic the adjective generally follows the noun: eg, 'Uisge Dubh' - Black Water; 'Tobermory' - Mary's Well.

Common Gaelic Elements in Place Names

Aber - *Confluence*
Abhainn - *River*
Achadh, Ach, Auch - *Field*
Allt - *Stream*
Aonach - *Steep slope*
Ard - *Promontory*
Bal, Ball - *Town, settlement*
Ban - *White, pale*
Beag, Beg - *Small*
Beinn, Ben - *Mountain*
Breac - *Speckled*
Buidhe - *Yellow*
Camas - *Bay*
Caol, Kyle - *Narrow*
Carn, Cairn - *Hill,
  heap of stones*
Ceann, Kin - *Head*
Clach - *Stone*
Cnoc - *Hillock*
Coille - *Wood*
Coire, Corrie - *Kettle, hollow*
Craggan - *Rocky hillock*

Creag, Craig - *Rock, cliff*
Croit, Croft - *Highland
  smallholding*
Dal, Dail - *Meadow*
Dearg - *Red*
Donn - *Brown*
Druim, Drum - *Ridge*
Dubh - *Black*
Dun - *Steep hill, fort*
Eas, Ess - *Waterfall*
Eilean - *Island*
Fionn - *White, fair*
Garbh - *Rough*
Geal - *White, bright*
Glas - *Grey, green*
Gleann, Glen - *Valley*
Gobhar, Gower - *Goat*
Gorm - *Blue*
Inver - *River mouth*
Kil - *Church*
Laggan - *Hollow*
Lairig - *Hill pass*

Leacann, Lechkin - *Slope*
Leitir, Letter - *Extensive slope*
Liath - *Grey*
Lochan - *Small loch*
Mor - *Large*
Ros - *Promontory*
Ruadh - *Red*
Rubha - *Point of land*
Sgeir - *Skerry*
Sgurr - *Peak, sharp top*
Strath - *Wide valley*
Sron - *Nose, point*
Stac - *Rocky column, cliff*
Stob - *Point, peak*
Stuc - *Pinnacle*
Tarbet - *Isthmus*
Tigh - *House*
Torr - *Mound, hill*
Tulach, Tullich - *Knoll*
Uaine - *Green*
Uamh - *Cave*
Uisge - *Water*

Natural History

This area can usefully be divided into a number of environments which recur along the routes - **Oak and other Broad-leaved Woodland, Commercial Forestry, Mountains and Moorland, Farmland, Freshwater** and **Seashore** - and the bird, animal and plant life typical of each can then be listed. This has been done below. Routes which particularly feature each environment are listed beside the headings. Naturally, it is impossible to be entirely accurate with such a brief study, and great good fortune is required to see some of the shyer species, but this should give a rough indication of the type of thing which may be seen along the way.

Oak and other Broad-leaved Woodland
(3,5,6,7, 8,10,11,18,25,27,30,37,38)
Following the ice age, and before man intervened, most of this area was covered by trees; **Scots pine** and **birch** on the poorer soils and the north facing slopes, and **oak** and

other broad-leaved trees on the better soils, the available flat land, and the south-facing slopes of the glens. These oak woods were particularly dense in Lorn. Further to the north they tended to be concentrated along the coastal fringe.

The trees were virtually all felled, for a variety of reasons, and now only fragments of the natural woodland remain. Of the oak woods, these are generally those areas which were managed during the 18th and 19th centuries to produce charcoal for the iron furnace at Bonawe. These woods were kept free of grazing animals, which destroy undergrowth and saplings.

The main remaining fragments are by Loch Awe *(37,38)*, Loch Creran, Glen Beasdale, in South Morar, and Loch Sunart *(6,7)*, with other patches along glens throughout the area. Some of these woods are now protected.

Apart from the **oak**, the woods can include **rowan, hazel, holly, alder, wych elm, birch** and **ash** where the soil is suitable. The floor of the wood tends to be mossy, with some grass, plus **blaeberry, primrose** and others. The oaks themselves tend to be swathed in mosses and lichens, and are often host to climbing **honeysuckle** and, less often, **ivy**.

The bird life in these woods is not great. Some **warblers** and **finches** may be seen, but the oak woods are generally very quiet places The shortage of small birds limits the range of birds of prey, although those which predominantly prey on small mammals (**buzzard** and **tawny owl**) are likely to be present.

The cover of the woods attracts larger mammals: **badger, hedgehog, stoat, weasel, wildcat, fox, roe deer** and, in the north of this area, the **pine marten**.

The woods are rich in insect life. The hills of the wood ant are common, as are many species of butterflies, beetles, moths. These in turn provide sustenance to a variety of species of bats.

Patches of other woodland can be found all over the area, but they tend to be restricted to rocky slopes and small, steep glens, where grazing animals cannot get at them. In low lying woods plant life can include **wood anemone, foxglove, bluebell, cow wheat, primrose, cranesbill** and **wood garlic**.

Commercial Forestry *(16,19,20,21,22,26, 28,32,39)*

These plantations are of comparatively little interest to naturalists. They provide cover for **rabbit, fox, roe deer** and others, but the trees are generally close together, thus keeping the sunlight from the forest floor and inhibiting the undergrowth neccesary to sustain the smaller mammals and insects at the bottom of the food chain.

The trees planted are quite varied. The list includes not only the native **Scots pine**, but also **lodge-pole pine; Sitka** and **Norway spruce; Japanese, European** and **hybrid larch; Douglas fir** and others; developed from the basic species to produce trees which grow straight and fast.

The bird life of the plantations can include **blue, great** and **coal tits, bullfinch** and **chaffinch, crossbill, siskin, jay** and **wood pigeon**. However, sightings can be difficult because of the close packed branches.

Mountains and Moorland *(1,4,12,13,16,17,18, 19,23,24,25,26,27,28,29,32,34,40)*

The Highlands are famous for their heather moors, which give a fine purple shade to the hillsides from July to September, but this ground cover is not universal on the hills of the western Highlands. In general, the densest occurrence of the heather moorland in this area is on the eastern side; on the hills and moors around 'Druim Alba' *(the Ridge of Scotland)* - Rannoch Moor, Glen Orchy, Glen Coe and Lochaber - the watershed between east and west. In this area the cover is generally of **ling heather, bearberry** and others.

In some areas the moors are 'floating' on a considerable depth of peat: a mass of black, sodden, half rotted vegetation, which provides effective fuel when dried. These peat moors tend to be very wet *(1,16,19,24)*, and pools and bogs of dark water often develop. These encourage plants such as **bog cotton, bog asphodel** and the pungent **bog myrtle**.

Where the heather cover is broken it gives way to a rocky grassland. This cover becomes more general to the west. The basalt rock of Mull, for instance, produces soils which are particularly suited to grasses.

The very highest peaks are rocky and virtually bare. The generally low temperatures and high winds maintain sub-alpine conditions, with pockets of snow lasting well into the summer on northern slopes. Some **ptarmigan**, the hardiest of the grouse family, may be seen near the tops, or lower in winter, but little else.

On the lower moors - which, in the west, tend to extend virtually to sea-level - **black** and **red grouse** are present, plus **stonechat, wheatear** and **curlew; peregrine, kestrel** and **golden eagle. Crows** are present here, as everywhere: predominantly the **hooded crow.**

The largest wild mammal in Britain is the **red deer.** These stay high in the hills during the summer - partly to escape the fierce insect life of the summer moors - but return to the lower moors during the winter. There are also local colonies of **sika deer** and **wild goats** (the descendants of domesticated animals), and carnivores such as the **wildcat, fox** and **stoat.** The **mountain hare** - which, like the **stoat** and the **ptarmigan,** turns white in the winter months - is rare in this area.

In addition to the above, most moors are heavily grazed by **sheep.**

Farmland *(31,33,36,40)*

In this area 'farmland' usually signifies low, better quality grassland; generally occurring by the coast, and given over to cattle grazing.

Bird and animal life tends to be a mixture of that of the woods, shore and moorland, with the addition of migrant species such as the **redwing** and **fieldfare.**

Freshwater *(1,3,5,11,18,19,21,38,39)*

This is rather a broad grouping, incorporating low level lochs, hill burns and moorland peat bogs. A great deal of water falls on the western Highlands, eventually reaching the sea via a teeming network of bogs, burns, ponds, falls, lochans, lochs and rivers, so most of the routes in this book pass likely habitats along the way. Only those routes where the water is a central feature are listed above.

The **bog cotton, asphodel** and **myrtle** and various mosses, reeds and grasses of the moors and peat bogs tend to follow the water courses to the sea's edge throughout this area; only being replaced by woodland flowers where the burns pass through high-sided, narrow glens, and trees have been able to grow. Various pondweeds, reeds and sedges grow by the lochs and lochans.

The most dramatic of the freshwater birds are the **red-throated** and **black-throated divers,** which nest by the high lochans; specifically chosen for their isolation. Also by the upper waters are **redshank, curlew** and **lapwing;** while **dipper** and **grey** and **pied wagtails** are common in the shaded glens.

There are few mammals which specifically live by the water, but one - the **otter** - is not uncommon throughout the area, although it is quite rare to see one. Other swimmers include **water vole** and **mink.**

Seashore *(2,8,9,10,11,14,15,27,30,31,35,36)*

The sea dominates the western side of this area, reaching far inland along the sea-lochs, and surrounding hundreds of islands. In general the foreshore is rocky, but in some places this gives way to salt-marshes and mud-flats, or to shell-sand beaches.

Rock type and boulder size have some effect on the life of the rocky foreshores, but the most important element is the degree of exposure to heavy seas. On exposed beaches the cover is limited to **lichens** and **barnacles,** while, in the sheltered lochs, there is a greater density of **sea-weeds,** plus **mussels** and **limpets. Crabs** are common between the high and low water marks, while **sea urchins** and **starfish** can be seen just below the lowest tides. The shells of **scallops** and other bivalves are often thrown up along the beaches.

Salt-marshes occur where streams or rivers have deposited alluvium, washed down from the hills, along the water's edge; forming a semi- stable grassland, riddled with winding channels and covered by the sea at high tide. This usually occurs at the sheltered heads of lochs. Below a certain point these become mud-flats; rich in **lugworms** and cockles, and thus attractive to waders such as the **curlew** and **oyster catcher.**

Shell-sand beaches occur on the exposed bays of Coll, Tiree, and the western promontories. They are backed by dunes (stabilised by **marram grass**), behind which is the machair: a band of grazing land, enriched by the shell-sand and additionally fertilised by manure and sea-weed.

The **common seal** is the sea mammal most likely to be seen; lying on rocky islands and points. In addition, **otters** can sometimes be seen swimming in the sea; particularly in the evenings.

Bird life includes a variety of **gulls (herring, common, black-headed, lesser black-back, greater black-back** and **kittiwake)** and **terns (common and arctic)**, plus **heron, razorbill, guillemot, puffin, cormorant** and **shag; mute** and **whooper swans; eider, teal, tufted duck, wigeon** and other ducks. Waders include **curlew, oyster catcher, dunlin, redshank, sandpiper** and others.

In addition, there has been a gradual increase in the number of **sea-eagles** along the coast; stemming from an original group released on Rum.

Advice to Walkers

Always check the weather forecast before setting off on the longer walks and prepare yourself accordingly. Remember that an excess of sunshine - causing sunburn or dehydration - can be just as debilitating as snow or rain, and carry adequate cover for your body in all conditions when on the hills.

Snow cover on the higher slopes often remains well into summer and should be avoided by inexperienced walkers as it often covers hidden watercourses and other pitfalls which are likely to cause injury. Also, when soft, snow is extremely gruelling to cross and can sap the energy very quickly. Walking on snow-covered hills should not be attempted without an ice-axe and crampons.

The other weather-associated danger on the hills is mist or low cloud - particularly common on these west Highland hills - which can appear very swiftly and cut visibility to a few yards. Such conditions should be anticipated, and a map and compass carried while on the higher ground.

Obviously these problems are unlikely to arise on the shorter, simpler routes, but it is always wise when out walking to anticipate the worst and to be ready for it. The extra equipment may never be needed, but it is worth taking anyway, just in case. Spare

food, a first-aid kit, a whistle and a torch with a spare battery should be carried on all hill walks. In addition, details of your route and expected time of return should be left with someone, whom you should advise on your safe return.

There is one final danger for hill walkers which is entirely predictable. From August onwards there is grouse shooting and deer stalking on the moors. If you are undertaking one of the hill routes then check with the local estate or tourist officer before doing so, thereby avoiding a nuisance for the sportsmen and possible danger to yourself.

Country Code

Guard against all risk of fire
Keep all dogs under proper control
    (especially during the lambing season - April/May)
Fasten all gates
Keep to the paths across farmland
Avoid damaging fences, hedges and walls
Leave no litter
Safeguard water supplies
Protect wildlife, wild plants and trees
Go carefully on country roads
Respect the life of the countryside

1 Loch Lundie

Length: 6 miles (9.5km)
Height Climbed: 450ft (140m)
Grade: B
Public conveniences: None
Public transport: Bus service between Fort William and Inverness

A series of rough tracks through the moorland and woodland surrounding a quiet hill loch.

Drive 26 miles north from Fort William through the Great Glen, on the A82 road to Inverness. At the point where the River Garry flows into Loch Oich is Invergarry; one time seat of the MacDonells of Invergarry whose ruined castle (burnt by the Duke of Cumberland after the Battle of Culloden) can be seen by the lochside. Just after the road crosses the river, turn left, up the A87, and look for a parking place to the left of the road, then walk on until a shop appears to the right.

    The path starts to the right of the shop. Go through a gate behind the buildings and follow a clear track up the side of the Aldernaig Burn; through mixed woodland, with a conifer plantation behind a fence to the left.

    Where the path joins another track cut right; crossing the burn by a bridge and continuing, across moorland, to a stand of conifers at the southern end of Loch Lundie. The path is quite clear, if rough; passing out of the trees and continuing through the damp moorland to the east of the loch.

    Once the track has curved round the head of the loch it cuts hard right. At this point turn left, onto another path, and continue along the foot of a slope, a little distance from the west side of the loch.

    The path eventually leaves the basin of Loch Lundie and, after crossing a low ridge and dropping down to ford Allt a'Bhainne *(the Milk Burn)*, joins another track, cutting along the edge of Glen Garry. Where the track forks cut right; down through Faichem camp site to a minor public road. Turn left along this to the junction with the A87; and then left again, for a short distance, to return to the shop.

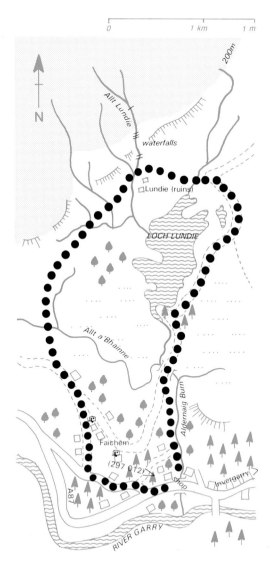

Walk 1

2 Mallaig

Length: 4 miles (6.5km)
Height climbed: 300ft (90m)
Grade: B
Public conveniences: Mallaig
Public transport: Rail service between Mallaig and Fort William

A short walk along the coast on public roads and a rough track; back over a low hill. Splendid views of the islands to the west.

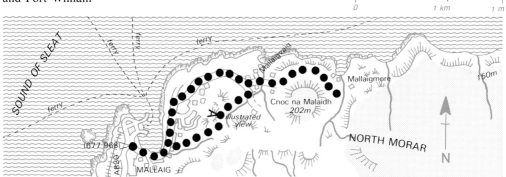

Mallaig is an important fishing harbour and a ferry terminus for Skye and the Small Isles. It is neither old (there was little on the site before this century) nor particularly pretty, but it has that vitality peculiar to working harbours, and occupies a most dramatic position on the edge of North Morar; looking out beyond the Hebrides to the Atlantic. The town is the northern terminus of the West Highland railway (running from Glasgow, through Fort William) and also marks the conclusion of the A830 road north from Fort William.

Park in Mallaig and walk around the head of the bay. Beyond the town continue around the point to the hamlet of Mallaigvaig. From here a rough path cuts along a steep slope, around the coast to the bay at Mallaigmore. From this track there are fine views across Loch Nevis to the mountains of Knoydart.

Double back to Mallaigvaig and follow the signposted track to the left, up a small glen, across a low pass and back down into Mallaig. To the right of this path there is a low hill, from which there are splendid views.

1. *Eigg* 2. *Mallaig* 3. *Rum* 4. *Sleat* 5. *Sound of Sleat* 6. *Cuillin Hills*

3 North Morar

Length: 8 miles (13.5km)
Height Climbed: Negligible
Grade: A
Public conveniences: Mallaig
Public transport: Morar Station on rail link
between Fort William and Mallaig

A long walk by the side of a large inland loch, on a quiet public road and a rough track. Back by the same route, or around the coast by ferry.

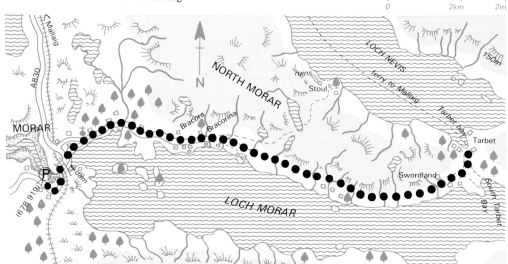

This walk makes use of an occasional ferry service, running from Mallaig, up Loch Nevis to Tarbet. If it is intended to use this for the return route then check ferry times (contact ferry operators through Mallaig Tourist Information Centre) and allow around 3 hours for the walk

To reach Morar, drive north on the A830 road from Fort William to Mallaig. Park in Morar, 2 miles south of Mallaig, beautifully situated by a white, sandy inlet across which the River Morar meanders.

Walk along the minor road to the east, by the north shore of Loch Morar. The loch is 17 miles long and, off Swordland, the water is over 1000ft deep. At the shallow western end there are a number of pleasant, wooded islands. On one of these there was a Catholic seminary, which was destroyed after the Battle of Culloden in 1746.

After 3 miles the road degenerates into a track, which quickly splits into two divergent paths. One leads over the hill to the north, to the little abandoned settlement of Stoul. The other (the path for this route) continues along the shore. The slope down to the water is very steep in places, and the rough path curves around the headlands above the loch, giving fine views of the mass of peaks at the eastern end of the loch, and westwards, across the wooded islands to the mountains of the island of Rum.

Continue on this path, past the Victorian shooting-lodge at Swordland. A short distance beyond the lodge the track splits. Cut hard left, through a narrow pass and down to the shore of Tarbet Bay on the sea-loch, Loch Nevis.

4 Glen Roy

Length: 5 miles (8km)
Height Climbed: 400ft (120m)
Grade: B
Public conveniences: None
Public transport: None

A brisk walk through an area of great geological interest. The going is generally rough, through the thick heather moorland on the hill sides.

The most interesting features of Glen Roy are its 'Parallel Roads': a series of sloping ridges, running the length of the glen at a uniform height. These were formed during the latter part of the ice age, when a loch formed in the glen, dammed by a glacier in Glen Spean. As the glacier deteriorated, over a long period, the loch was held at different levels. The parallel roads mark the beaches which formed along the strand of this loch. This route follows the line of one such strand.

To reach Glen Roy drive north from Fort William on the A82. Turn onto the A86 at Spean Bridge and drive 3 miles to Roybridge. Turn left at the village, up Glen Roy. There is a car park 3 miles up the glen.

A rough path runs directly up the slope of Bohuntine Hill behind the car park, across the lowest of the parallel roads, at 857ft/261m, and on up to the next at 1068ft/326m. From here the lines of the roads are visible along the sides of the upper glen.

Walk north along the road, turning sharply around the northern end of Bohuntine Hill and continuing along the damp slopes of Glen Collarig. The line of the road disappears along this section, and at the southern end of the hill there are large conifer plantations. Cut up to the left at the conifers, across the level moorland of Meall Dubh, and down the far side to rejoin the parallel road. Follow this back to the car park.

One famous visitor to the glen was the Marquess of Montrose, who, at the height of his brief, brilliant career, led a small Royalist army over the snow-filled passes at the head of the glen in 1645, on his way to surprise and defeat the Duke of Argyll at Inverlochy.

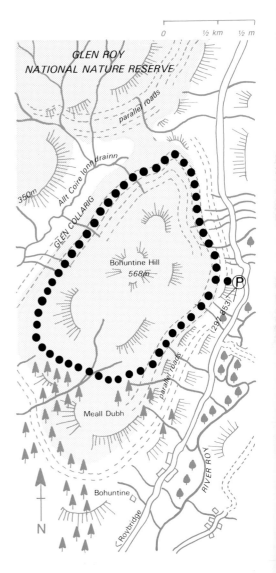

5 Caledonian Canal

Length: 4 miles (7km)
Height Climbed: Negligible
Grade: B
Public conveniences: None
Public transport: Bus service from Fort William

A leisurely stroll along a canal towpath, and back along a quiet public road. Fine view of Ben Nevis.

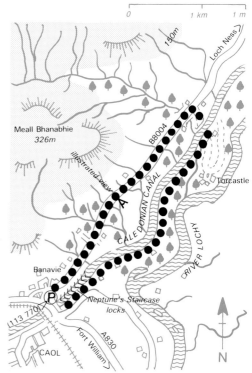

The Caledonian Canal was surveyed by Thomas Telford at the start of the 19th century, and finally completed in 1847; shortening the long trip around Scotland's north coast. The canal runs from Inverness, on the Moray Firth, to Corpach, just north of Fort William. It was intended as an aid to fishing and trading vessels, but is now largely used by pleasure craft.

Drive north from Fort William and turn left onto the road to Mallaig; then right, after crossing the canal, into the car park at Banavie.

At this point the canal climbs through a series of locks known as 'Neptune's Staircase'. Start walking up the eastern side of the canal.

After 2 miles a path drops down from the towpath, just before some cottages to the right of the canal. Turn down this and double back through a charming arch beneath the canal. Where this path joins the B8004 turn left to return to Banavie. Along this road there are tremendous views to the south-east of Ben Nevis and the surrounding peaks.

1. *Aonach Mór (1219m)* 2. *Carn Mór Dearg (1223m)* 3. *Ben Nevis (1344m)*
4. *Carn Dearg (1211m)* 5. *Meall an t-Suidhe (708m)* 6. *Mullach nan Coirean (938m)*
7. *Cow Hill* 8. *Inverlochy Castle Hotel* 9. *Caledonian Canal* 10. *Aluminium Works*

6 Ariundle

Length: 4 miles (6.5km)
Height Climbed: 350ft (100m)
Grade: C
Public conveniences: Strontian
Public transport: Occasional bus service from
Fort William

*Short, lineal route through a natural oak-
wood. Paths good.*

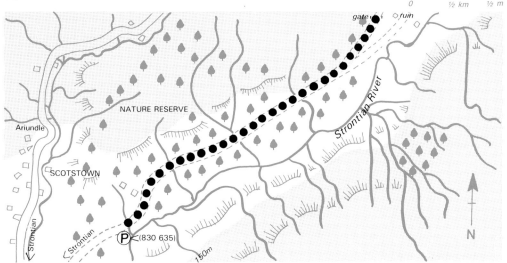

Strontian and the straggling line of
settlements spreading 2 miles up the valley to
the north were built to house the miners in
the local lead mines, first brought into
production in the early 18th century. The
village gave its name to Strontium, a metal
found in the mineral Strontianite, first
discovered in the lead mines. The mines are
closed now (their remains can still be seen
beside the road to Polloch) but the hills
behind Strontian hold another valuable
commodity: a Highland oak wood, of the
type which once covered much of the western
Highlands.

To reach Strontian drive south from Fort
William to Corran Ferry, on the A82. Take
the ferry across the narrows and then turn
left, down the A861, for 13 miles to
Strontian, at the head of the long inlet of
Loch Sunart. Turn right at the north end of

the village, up a minor road. After 1 mile the
road forks. Follow the right-hand track, ½ mile
to the car park.

The route is clear: along a good track on
the side of the glen of the Strontian River and
back by the same route, through an area now
maintained as a Nature Reserve. The wood is
largely of oak trees, swathed in a rich mass of
mosses and lichens, but there are also birch,
rowan, ash, alder and others. Typically, for a
northern oak wood, the wood is very quiet;
rich in insects but poor in birds. The
mammals present include otter, fox, wild cat,
pine marten and roe deer; only the latter of
which is likely to be seen.

This wood owes its survival to the
management of the charcoal burners of the
18th and 19th centuries, who supplied oak
charcoal for the iron works on Loch Etive.

7 Oakwood Trail

Length: 1 mile (2km)
Height Climbed: Negligible
Grade: C
Public conveniences: None
Public transport: None

A short, signposted walk through natural woodland on a promontory above a sea-loch. Fine views of the surrounding hills. Paths clear.

This is a very short walk, through a patch of oakwood to the east of Salen Bay.

To reach Salen, drive south from Fort William to Corran Ferry; take the ferry across the narrow neck of Loch Linnhe and turn left along the A861. It is 23 miles along this road to the little village; built around the head of an inlet of Loch Sunart, at the junction of the A861 with the B8007 Ardnamurchan road.

A little before the village there is a small car park beside the road. Park here and start walking along a clear track. The route follows a short loop, passing a viewpoint on the promontory above Salen Bay and doubling back to the car park. The views are dramatic and extensive: down Loch Sunart and across the water to the hills of Morvern.

The cover in this wood is broad-leaved and predominantly of oak trees; a type of woodland which once clothed the south-facing slopes of most of the west Highland glens. There is comparatively little bird life in these woods, but they are rich in mosses, lichens and insects. Plant life includes honeysuckle, primrose, wood anemone and cow wheat.

There is a variety of animal life in the oakwoods, but it is generally either small - mice, voles and shrews - or largely nocturnal, such as the fox, wild cat, badger and pine marten. The only mammals which are likely to be seen are roe deer - particularly early in the morning - or, in the evening, the bats which feed on the wide variety of insects which inhabit the oak woods.

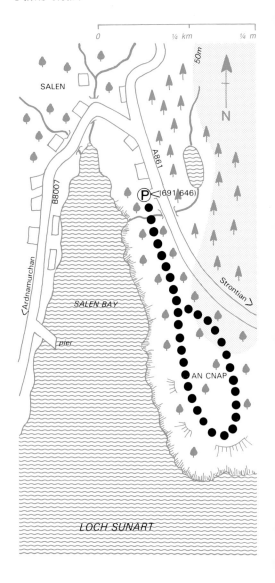

8 Castle Tioram

Length: 4 miles (6.5km)
Height Climbed: 500ft (150m)
Grade: B
Public conveniences: None
Public transport: None

A varied walk, through rhododendrons and woodland by a sea-loch, and across an interior of heather moorland. Paths of varying quality.

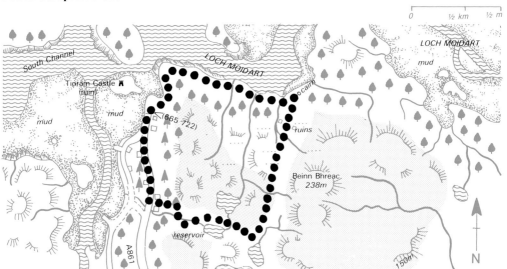

Built in the 14th century, Castle Tioram was the stronghold of the MacDonalds of Clanranald. It was never taken, which is scarcely surprising since it occupies a position of great strength: on a small mound on the mud flats of Loch Moidart, which becomes an island at high tide. The building was partially destroyed by Clanranald in 1715 to keep it from the hands of the Campbells when he left to join the Jacobite rebellion.

To reach Tioram, drive north from Fort William on the Inverness road, and turn onto the A830 to Mallaig. At Lochailort turn onto the A861, and follow it round the head of muddy Loch Moidart; turning right, just before reaching Acharacle, on a minor road signposted to the castle.

Park by the road verge, opposite the building, and start walking along the coast.

The path, through mixed woodland and rhododendrons, is overgrown in places, but quite clear, and provides fine views of the wooded islands in the loch.

After rounding the point, continue for 1 mile, round the head of a little bay, before cutting right at a small cairn, onto a faint path. This climbs up by a small burn, through a wood of oak and birch, to some ruined crofts at the edge of the woodland. Continue climbing across the moorland beyond these.

After a short distance the path drops down to a pair of small lochans. Turn right before the first of these, and cut through a narrow gap; past a small reservoir and down a narrow, wooded glen to the road. From this path there are fine views across the mouth of Loch Moidart to the islands of Muck and Eigg.

9 Sanna to Portuairk

Length: 2 miles (3km) there and back
Height Climbed: 150ft (40m)
Grade: B
Public conveniences: None
Public transport: None

A short walk through coastal moorland and sand dunes. Possible extensions. Rough in places.

The promontory of Ardnamurchan is some 18 miles long, from the little village of Salen on Loch Sunart to the the headland ot Corrachadh Mòr: the most westerly point of mainland Britain. To anyone uninitiated in the joys of Highland, single-track roads it will seem every inch of this distance and more, as the road winds through the great empty expanses of rocky moorland. Leave plenty of time for the trip.

To reach Ardnamurchan follow the Mallaig road from Fort William and turn south, onto the A861, as far as Salen. At this point turn onto the B8007. Follow the signs for Sanna; a small crofting community by a wide sandy bay near the point of Ardnamurchan.

In the midst of such a vast, empty area there scarcely seems any point in mentioning a single route; the area is so clearly perfect for long hill walks. Indeed, outside the stalking season, when it is best to stay off the hills, there is no reason why well-equipped, experienced walkers should not set off at almost any point. However, the coast along this stretch has developed into a number of pleasant sandy bays, and the views across the water - of Coll to the south-east; Muck, Eigg and Rum to the north-west - are tremendous.

Park at Sanna and walk south, through the dunes. To the left is Meall Sanna; not high, but craggy and, like much of Ardnamurchan, largely scraped free of soil by the glaciers of the ice age.

Where the beach ends cut inland over a rocky ridge, then drop down again - there is no clear path - across a small burn surrounded by wild iris, and on into the hamlet of Portuairk.

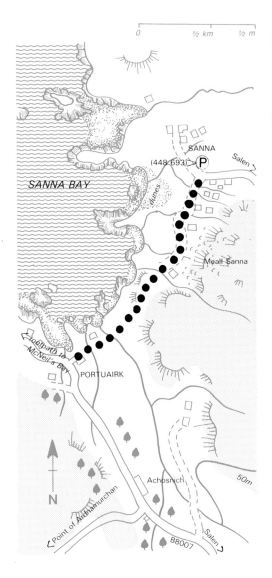

10 Rubha nan Gall

Length: 3 miles (5km) there and back
Height Climbed: 170ft (50m)
Grade: C
Public conveniences: Tobermory
Public transport: Bus services from Dervaig and Craignure

A short, lineal walk on a good path; through mixed woodland on a steep slope above the sea.

This is a relatively short, simple walk along the shore to the north of Tobermory Bay, but the path has great character and the views are excellent.

Tobermory is a planned village. Building was started at the end of the 18th century to create a fishing station as a centre for the burgeoning herring fishery. During the 19th century this was a huge industry and attracted hundreds of boats. In time the herring disappeared, but Tobermory remained and, following a period of neglect, is now in excellent condition. Its harbour, lined with brightly coloured buildings, is one of the handsomest on the coast.

Start walking from the ferry terminal at the north end of the bay. Beyond the town a hill slopes steeply to the water. The path climbs onto this slope, cuts round a headland and continues northwards through mixed woodland. The flowers by the path include speedwell, primrose, foxglove, bluebell, wild strawberries, potentilla, cranesbill and banks of pungent wood garlic.

The path cuts out of the woodland and continues along the coast. Excellent views now open up: north to Ardnamurchan, with the ruin of Mingary Castle clearly visible by the shore; and east to the mouth of Loch Sunart and the hills of Morvern. There is a view indicator by the path which identifies the various features.

The path ends at the lighthouse on Rubha nan Gall *(the Point of the Strangers)*, built in the mid 19th century. Beyond this is Bloody Bay where, in the late 15th century, a sea battle was fought between John, Lord of the Isles, and his son, Angus.

Return by the same route.

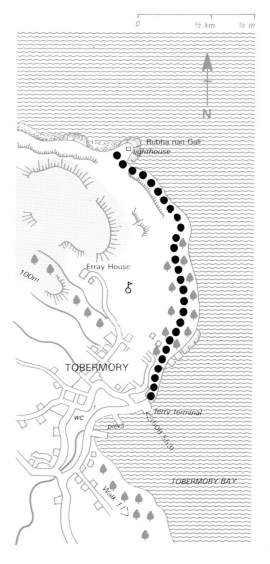

11 Aros

Length: 4 miles (6.5km)
Height Climbed: Negligible
Grade: B
Public conveniences: Tobermory
Public transport: Bus services to Tobermory from Dervaig and Craignure

A short walk through a steep slope of mixed woodland above Tobermory Bay, leading to wooded parkland and a small ornamental loch. Paths good.

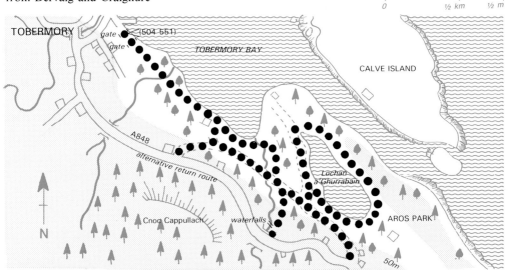

Start walking from the water front in Tobermory. Walk south, along the edge of the bay, past the garage to a gate by a small cottage. Go through this gate, past the cottage, and through another gate beyond. Be sure to shut these gates behind you.

The path now runs through dense, mixed woodland, clustered on a steep slope running down to Tobermory Bay. Tobermory is an excellent natural harbour; facing east onto the narrow Sound of Mull, and protected by Calve Island. It was this sheltered bay which encouraged the British Fisheries Society to build the original fishing station here in the late 18th century. Nowadays the bay is very popular with cruising yachts, which fill the anchorage during the summer months.

Two hundred years before the town was founded a Spanish galleon - thought to be the Florida - was storm-bound in the bay following the débâcle of the Armada in 1588. For some reason the Spaniards and the Macleans of Mull argued and the ship was sunk. Since then the galleon has been the object of many dives. A cannon raised from the wreck is now kept at Duart Castle, in the south of the island.

The path continues along the shore to the woods and rhododendrons of Aros Park, through which there are a number of paths. At its heart is Lochan a'Ghurrabain: an ornamental loch, surrounded by trees and rimmed with water-lilies. Elsewhere there are paths by the burn which runs through the park; passing two sets of waterfalls.

Either return by the same route or follow one of the tracks to the A848 and turn right, back into Tobermory.

12 'S Airde Beinn

Length: 2 miles (3km)
Height Climbed: 450ft (140m)
Grade: C
Public conveniences: None
Public transport: Bus service between
Tobermory and Dervaig

*A short, lineal hill climb to a small loch
in an extinct volcanic crater. Excellent
views.*

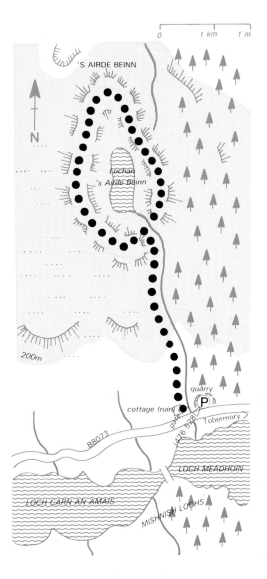

The island of Mull is almost entirely
composed of basalt, granite and other igneous
rocks; the product of great volcanic activity in
the distant past. One obvious relic of this
period of upheaval is the little basalt crater of
'S Airde Beinn at the northern end of the
island.

To reach the hill, drive west from
Tobermory on the B8073. After 1 mile the
road reaches a large conifer plantation on the
right-hand side. A short distance before the
end of the plantation, as the road passes to
the right of little Loch Meadhoin *(Middle
Loch),* the central of the three linked
Mishnish Lochs, a small quarry opens up to
the right of the road.

Park in the quarry and walk a short
distance down the road to a ruined cottage.
Go through the gate beside the ruin and start
walking up the faint path beyond, by the side
of a burn.

At first the path crosses grassland, but
this gradually gives way to heather moorland,
dotted with bog cotton and bog asphodel.

After an easy climb of ½ mile the burn cuts
through a narrow gap. Pass through this into
the crater, the centre of which is filled by a
small lochan.

Climb up onto the surrounding ridge and
walk around the rim of the crater. From this
point there are splendid views: east to
Tobermory Bay with Morvern beyond; north-
east to the mouth of Loch Sunart; north to
the point of Ardnamurchan, with Canna and
the hills of Rum beyond; and west to the low
island of Coll. A splendid view.

13 Speinne Mór

Length: 5 miles (9km)
Height Climbed: 1000ft (300m)
Grade: A
Public conveniences: None
Public transport: Bus service between Tobermory and Dervaig

A brisk hill climb. Paths unclear, but walking easy. Splendid views in all directions.

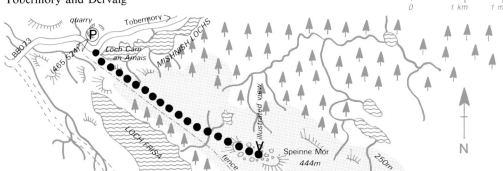

Speinne Mór, though small compared to Mull's highest peak (Ben More, in the south of the island) is high enough to overlook the northern hills, and to provide fine views.

To reach the hill, drive west from Tobermory on the B8073. Near the end of Loch Carn an Amais, the most westerly of the three Mishnish Lochs, there is a small quarry to the right of the road. Park in the quarry and start walking up the ridge to the south of the loch.

There is no particular path, and the going is rough, steep and damp in places, but the route is easy enough. After ½ mile the ground flattens out and there is a view of Loch Frisa to the south. Follow an old fence along this stretch and then, when the ground starts to rise again, leave the fence and head straight for the summit. On the upper slopes the cover is of cropped grass over dark basaltic soil; littered with larger rocks. Ideal for walking.

The round view from the summit includes Coll and the Treshnish Isles to the west, Ben More to the south, the Sound of Mull and Morvern beyond to the east and north (see illustration) to Ardnamurchan and the islands beyond.

1. *Ardnamurchan* 2. *Ben Hiant (528m)* 3. *Tobermory* 4. *Loch Sunnart* 5. *Sound of Mull* 6. *Morvern*

14 Ulva

Length: Up to 10 miles (16km) or more
Height Climbed: Up to 350ft (110m)
Grade: A/B/C
Public conveniences: None
Public transport: Ferry from Oskamull, Mull.

A number of tracks and rough footpaths across a quiet island off Mull's west coast.

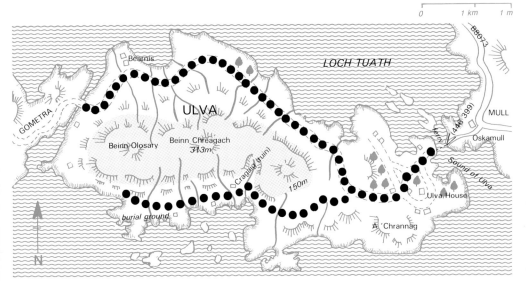

Ulva is a quiet, peaceful island - 5 miles long and 2 miles wide at its broadest point - lying just off Mull's west coast; formed entirely of volcanic rocks, shaped by the glaciers of the ice age. The end result is a rocky island, rising steeply to over 1000ft, but ringed by a relatively flat raised beach on which the island's houses are built and crops are grown.

Ulva is privately owned, and there are no cars on the island, but visitors are permitted to explore on foot, and a number of paths are signposted on the island.

To reach Ulva, drive south from Tobermory on the A848 as far as Salen. Turn onto the B8035 for 2 miles, and then onto the B8073, along Loch na Keal, for 7 miles to Oskamull. Turn down a minor road to the jetty from which a little ferry crosses the narrow Sound of Ulva.

On the flat land at the east end of the island, surrounded by a considerable amount of mature, mixed woodland, are Ulva House and a church designed by the great engineer Thomas Telford. Further west the island becomes wilder, and views open up of the surrounding islands.

The southern path leads over a ridge of moorland and down to a ruined mill at Cragaig, at the head of a rocky inlet. On the promontory beyond the inlet is a burial ground of the McQuarries, who lived on this island from the 13th century to the latter part of the 18th. Off shore is Little Colonsay, with the islands of Staffa and the Dutchman's Cap beyond.

The northern path leads the length of the island. A leaflet describing all these routes in detail is available at the ferry.

15 Iona

Length: Up to 10 miles (16km)
Height Climbed: Up to 350ft (100m)
Grade: A/B/C
Public conveniences: Iona, Fionnphort
Public transport: Ferrys from Fionnphort on
Mull and Oban. Bus service from Craignure

*A number of public roads, tracks and
rough footpaths across this famous island
off the west coast of Mull.*

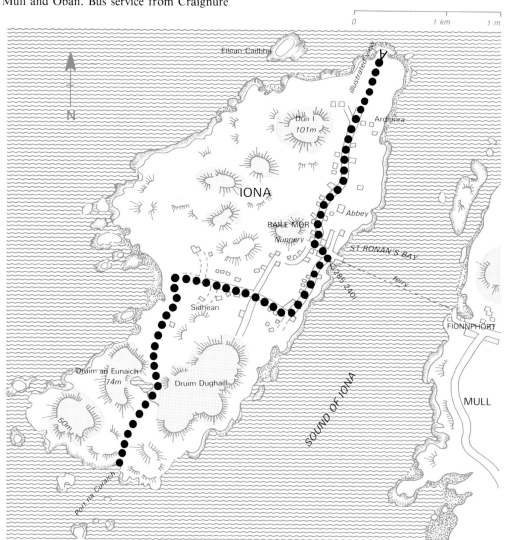

Iona is a small, low sandstone island, sitting to the west of the Ross of Mull - a long finger of basalt and granite pointing out into the Atlantic at the southern end of the island. Its scenery is rocky, yet green and fertile on the machair, and fringed - particularly at the northern end - by white sands.

Walking is generally easy; along metalled roads and across low, cropped grassland or open beaches, but there is one short climb - to the summit of Dun I (332ft), Iona's highest point - and some rougher walking through the lumpy terrain at the southern end of the island.

Iona's position ensures fine views of the scattered Inner Hebrides. East to the indented coastline of Mull, with the peak of Ben More prominent; north to Staffa, Ulva, Rum and the Treshnish Islands; further west to Coll and Tiree, and south to Islay and the distinctive hills of Jura.

To reach Iona from Tobermory, drive south on the A848 to Salen, and then continue along the A849, around the south-eastern corner of the island and along the Ross to Fionnphort: the ferry terminus for the short trip (less than 1 mile) across the Sound of Iona.

Iona is an extremely popular destination for visitors, but they tend to stay within sight of the pier, and the remainder of the island is quiet enough.

The visitors come partly for the scenery, but more particularly for the unique place which Iona holds in the religious and political history of Scotland, and for the island's famous tranquility. How much of the latter is it possible to experience around St Ronan's Bay in July is questionable, but the history is still tangible enough in the ecclesiastical buildings on the eastern side of the island.

Iona's importance is entirely due to St Columba; an Irish prince who came to the island in AD 563 (his landing place was Port na Curraigh at the south of the island) and founded a religious community, with the intention of spreading Christianity to the pagan Picts who inhabited most of Scotland at that time. In this he was entirely successful, and achieved, besides, a lasting veneration for the site of his community despite its peripheral location. Throughout the subsequent centuries a great many kings (not only Scottish, but also Irish and Norwegian) and local chiefs were buried on this, the most holy of sites, and by the 8th century Iona had become one of the great religious and cultural centres of Europe.

All this achievement was jeopardised by the attacks of the vikings (to which Iona, in its isolated position, was particularly vulnerable) during the late 8th, 9th and 10th centuries. In one attack 68 monks were killed, near the current landing place.

A similar destruction occurred during the Reformation, when the Abbey and a great many of the surviving relics were destroyed, but the building has since been repaired and re-roofed. The island is now owned by the National Trust for Scotland.

1. *Dutchman's Cap* 2. *Treshnish Islands* 3. *Rum* 4. *Staffa* 5. *Ulva* 6. *Mull*

16 Peat Road

Length: 5 miles (8km)
Height climbed: 725ft (220m)
Grade: B
Public conveniences: Fort William
Public transport: Bus and rail services to Fort William from all directions

A brisk hill crossing; back by quiet public roads. Fine views of Ben Nevis. Paths rough but clear.

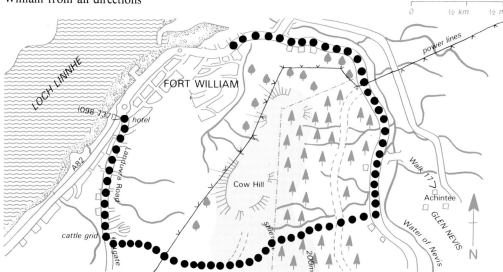

Start walking from Fort William. At the southern end of High Street there is a roundabout, by the West End Hotel. Turn into Landuvra Road, and start walking up the hill, through a built up area.

At the end of the houses there is a cattle-grid and, just beyond that, a gate to the left of the road. Start walking along the rough but clear track beyond the gate; slowly climbing across heather moorland, dotted with bog cotton, clumps of reeds and the occasional birch tree. This moorland sits on deposits of peat - a deep layer of sodden, black, half-rotted vegetation, which, when cut and dried, can be burnt like coal. This path was originally formed by people climbing to the moor to cut or collect the peats.

As the path rises there are views ahead of Ben Nevis and of the pointed peaks of

Killichonate Forest to its right. Looking back down the path there are views along Loch Linnhe to the islands of Lismore and Mull.

Carry on along the track until it reaches a small cairn. At this point the original track cuts hard left, up Cow Hill, and a rough footpath cuts off to the right. Follow this, across the moor to a large forestry plantation on the west side of Glen Nevis. Cross a stile to enter the plantation.

The path drops down through the forest, crosses a broad track, and continues beyond it, down to the road. Looking up to the head of the glen there is a fine view of the dramatic peaks of Mamore Forest.

Turn left, down the quiet public road, to the A82; then left again to return to Fort William.

17 Ben Nevis

Length: Up to 11 miles (18km) to summit and back
Height climbed: 4400ft (1330m)
Grade: A
Public conveniences: None
Public transport: None

A rough, gruelling hill climb up Britain's highest peak. Views outstanding, weather permitting.

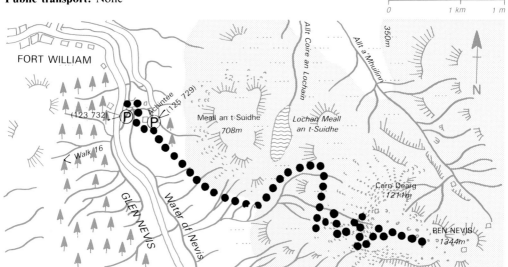

To reach the foot of the path up Ben Nevis drive north from the centre of Fort William and then cut right to follow one of the two minor roads up Glen Nevis. There are car parks on either (see map).

The great, rounded granite mass of Ben Nevis is the highest hill in Great Britain, and, during the summer, a large number of people trek slowly along the path up its west ridge. Sadly, it is not the most fascinating of climbs, and the doleful procession of walkers along the long incline gives the impression of a mass act of penitence. Nonetheless, it is a pleasant thing to have done, and the views - when they can be seen - are superb.

A few points should be made about the climb. Firstly, do make sure that you are sensibly attired for the conditions at the top of the hill, as well as for those at the bottom.

Its very height ensures that it will be cold (even in mid-summer there are often pockets of snow near the summit) and the omnipresent wind adds to the chill. In addition, the path is very rough and it is foolish not to wear thick hill-walking boots for the climb. On those rare days when the peak is free of cloud it is still important to keep covered up: at this height the sun burns very easily.

There should be no trouble following the path, which cuts deeply into the hillside below Meall an t-Suidhe, but be aware that the round contours of the southern face are not repeated to the north, where there are cliffs of well over 1000ft, and be sure to stick to the path (marked by a series of cairns across the rocky ground near the summit) in thick weather.

18 Glen Nevis

Length: Up to 30 Miles (48km), to Corrour and back
Height climbed: 350ft (100m), to Steall
Grade: A/B/C
Public conveniences: None
Public transport: None

A long, lineal track; leading through a narrow, wooded gorge to a broad, flat, upper valley. Tremendous scenery.

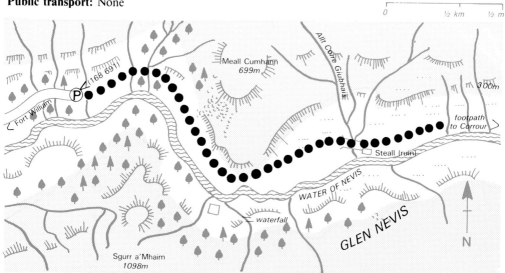

This is a long, lineal route which leads, ultimately, to Corrour Station (but only after a gruelling trek which should not be attempted without detailed maps, etc). Perhaps the most dramatic scenery, however, is along the first two miles (ie, as far as the ruin at Steall).

To reach the walk, drive to the northern end of Fort William and follow the signs for Glen Nevis. A quiet road leads up, through this narrow glen, hemmed in by tall hills and with a scattering of woodland along the river, to a car park at the end of the road. To the north of the car park sheets of water run down the smooth rock face of a southern spur of Ben Nevis. A sign indicates the start of the path.

The track is quite clear, running along the side of a wooded gully through which the Water of Nevis pours, zig-zagging between Meall Cumhann and the northern buttress of

Sgurr a'Mhaim. The wood – of Scots pine, birch, sallow, rowan and others – is thick on the steep slopes, and the path runs along a narrow ledge; sometimes overhung by cliffs. At first the river can only be heard, rumbling amongst the rocks below, but further on. where it rises to the level of the path, the way in which the cliffs and rocks have been carved by the water can be seen.

The gorge lasts for about ¹/₂ mile, after which the path rounds an outcrop of rock and a broader glen, through which the river slowly meanders, comes to view. Down the hill on the far side of the glen there is an impressive waterfall.

The path becomes less clear now, and the going damper. The trees end and the moorland begins. Walk as far as you wish and then double back to the car park.

19 Loch Ossian

Length: 9 miles (14.5km)
Height climbed: Negligible
Grade: A
Public conveniences: None
Public transport: Station on Glasgow-Fort William rail link; no roads across the moor

A flat walk on clear paths, across moorland and through forestry, around a secluded inland loch surrounded by hills.

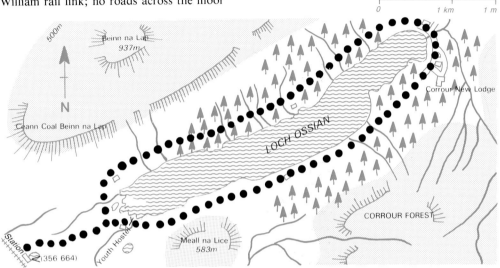

Rannoch Moor is a mass of lumpy moorland on the Perthshire/Argyll border; covered with meandering burns and shallow lochans, bedded into the black, sodden peat. The main body of the moor is to the south, between Lochs Laidon and Tulla and the mouth of Glen Coe, but an arm of undulating moorland stretches northwards, up to Corrour Station. There is no road to the station.

Start walking from Corrour, following the path which runs towards the Youth Hostel at Loch Ossian across the moorland to the east of the station. During the ice age Rannoch Moor was a basin of ice, from which glaciers spilled out in every direction, grinding down the valleys which radiate from the moor. Rannoch is still littered with the debris which was deposited when the ice melted.

Looking back from the track there is a fine view of the peak of Leum Uilleim, behind its broad corrie. To the north are the hills around Loch Trieg, with the Munros around Loch Ossian to the east.

After 1 mile the loch comes to view; surrounded by peaks and with a fringe of conifers around its far end.

The path is very clear; along the edge of the loch: across moorland initially and then through conifers - the plantations of Sir John Stirling Maxwell, who pioneered Highland forestry during the early part of this century.

Double back down the far side and return to the station. Be sure to leave enough time to finish the walk in time to catch a return train. Three hours is a comfortable time in which to complete the route.

20 Corrychurrachan

Length: 2 miles (3km)
Height climbed: 200ft (70m)
Grade: C
Public conveniences: None
Public transport: None

A short, signposted forestry trail on clear tracks. Views of upper Loch Linnhe.

This is a staight-forward forest walk, along Forestry Commission tracks through thick conifer plantations which are planted along the lower slopes of the most westerly hills of Lochaber, butted against the shore of Loch Linnhe: a long sea-inlet which stretches from Fort William down to Mull. From the high section of this path there are good views across upper Loch Linnhe to shallow Inverscaddle Bay, backed by the hills of Ardgour. Down the loch are the Corran narrows, across which the car ferry runs to Ardgour, Morvern and Ardnamurchan.

To reach Corrychurrachan from Fort William, head south from the town on the A82 road, and drive 6 miles along Loch Linnhe until a sign indicates a car park for the walk, up to the left.

Walk north out of the car park and follow a broad track through the trees along the steep side of Beinn Bhan. After a short distance a rough path leads up to the right, zig-zagging through young trees to join another track, further up the hill.

Turn right along this track, which eventually doubles back to the car park.

21 The Lochan

Length: 2 miles (3km)
Height climbed: Negligible
Grade: C
Public conveniences: Glencoe village
Public transport: Bus service from Oban and
Fort William

*A short forest trail through mixed
woodland around a small loch. Fine
views of surrounding mountain and
coastal scenery.*

The Lochan trail provides a number of short
paths through a very pleasant and varied
conifer and broad-leaved plantation, with a
track around a small lochan, and good views
(see below) from vantage points above Loch
Leven. The paths are very clear and generally
dry.

To reach the walk drive to Glencoe
village - at the western end of Glen Coe, on
the A82 Fort William to Glasgow road - and
follow the main street, eastwards, over the
bridge across the River Coe. Just beyond the
bridge turn left, up the drive to the hospital.
When the drive forks take the right-hand
track, which leads up to the car park.

To the east of the plantation is the
prominent mound of Sgurr na Ciche, the Pap
of Glen Coe; the most westerly peak on the
north side of the glen. To the west the views
down Loch Leven are extensive. In the loch
there are two small islands. The wooded
island is Eilean Munde *(the Island of Mundis)*
on which there are the remains of a church.
The grassy island is Eilean Choinneich *(the
Island of Meetings)* and was a neutral meeting
place where clan disputes were resolved.

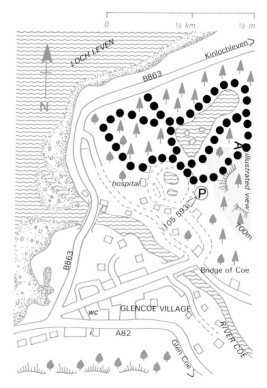

1. *Sgorr Dhearg (1024m)* 2. *Ballachulish* 3. *Creag Ghorm* 4. *Loch Leven*
5. *Creach Bheinn (853m)* 6. *Garbh Bheinn (885m)* 7. *Loch Linnhe* 8. *Ballachulish Bridge*
9. *Eilean Munde* 10. *Eilean Choinneich* 11. *Creag Bhreac*

22 Signal Rock

Length: 1½ miles (2.5km)
Height climbed: Negligible
Grade: C
Public conveniences: Information centre
Public transport: None

A number of clear, signposted tracks through mixed woodland in the heart of mountainous Glen Coe.

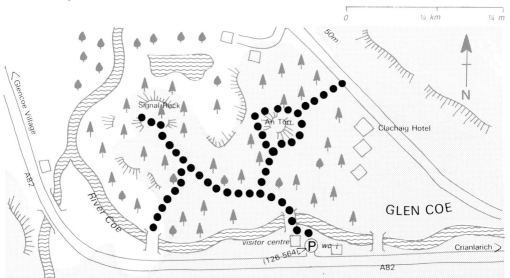

Signal Rock sits amongst the woods in a crook in the River Coe, where Glen Coe bends to the north, about 2 miles south-east of Glencoe village. From the top of this abrupt, rocky hillock can be seen (or could be seen, before the trees grew up around it) the greater part of the glen. This useful vantage point was used by the people of the glen as a signal station. Also, it is traditionally believed to be the point from which the command was given - most probably by lighting a large bonfire - at the start of the Massacre of Glen Coe, on the morning of 14th February, 1692.

The cold-blooded murder of the MacDonalds of Glen Coe by their guests - soldiers of the Duke of Argyll's regiment; commanded by Robert Campbell of Glen Lyon, and under the orders of King William - is one of the most reprehensible and depressing acts in British history.

There is an information centre in the glen, from which the walk to the loch begins. The paths, largely through conifers, with some broad-leaved woodland interspersed, are clearly signposted and provide dry walking.

The scenery in this area is some of the most dramatic in the Highlands; with towering, steep, rocky peaks surrounding the narrow glen. To the north of the rock is Sgurr nam Fiannaidh *(the Peak of the Fiann)*; a reference to the legendary Irish warriors who fought under Finn MacCumhaill, and who are associated, in old tales, with many places throughout the Highlands. To the south is the broad Gleann Leac na Muidhe and the grey faces of An t-Sròn *(the Nose)* and Aonach Dubh *(Black Slope)*, on which is Ossian's Cave; traditionally believed to have been the retreat of Finn's bardic son.

23 Devil's Staircase

Length: 6 miles (9.5km) one way
Height climbed: 1800ft (550m) north to south;
900ft (270m) south to north
Grade: A
Public conveniences: Kinlochleven
Public transport: Kinlochleven to Glencoe bus

An old track across moor-covered hills. The route is generally clear and there are excellent views of the surrounding hills.

The 'Devil's Staircase' is the name given to a steep, zig-zagging section of the hill-path leading from the eastern end of Glen Coe to Kinlochleven to the north. The path was originally a military road, built in the mid-18th century as part of the grand plan for the supression of the Highlands after the Jacobite uprisings.

Park at Altnafeadh; across the River Coupall from the great bulk of Buachaille Etive Mór; the hill which marks the eastern entrance to Glen Coe from Rannoch Moor. The path is signposted and starts just to the west of Altnafeadh, climbing slowly across damp moorland before the slope steepens approaching the col between Stob Eoin Mhic Mhartuin and Beinn Bheag. The track then cuts back and forth across the slope, quickly climbing to the dip between the hills, from where there are splendid views of the rugged peaks to the south, and a distant sighting of the rounded bulk of Ben Nevis, across the hills of Mamore Forest to the north.

The track now crosses a wide heathery corrie and cuts round a low ridge before dropping again to cross Allt Coire Odhair-mhóir. To the east the Blackwater Reservoir is visible. This is the main power source for the aluminium works at Kinlochleven. Down in the narrow glen of the River Leven there is extensive broad-leaved woodland.

The path joins a more permanent track and drops down towards the town, making a wide detour to cross the bridge over the Allt Coire Mhorair. To the right, alongside this final section, are the great pipes which carry the water down to the works.

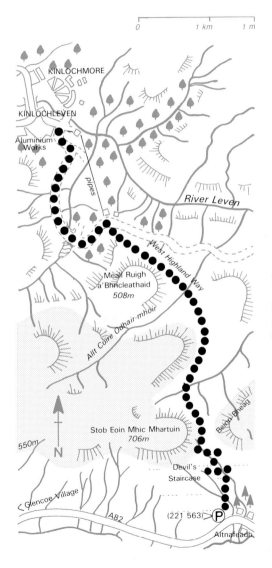

24 Glen Coe to Glen Etive

Length: 9½ miles (15km)
Height climbed: 800ft (240m) south through
L. Eilde; 1300ft (400m) north through L. Gartain
Grade: A
Public conveniences: None
Public transport: None

A long, rough, steep path through two narrow passes. Excellent mountain and moorland scenery.

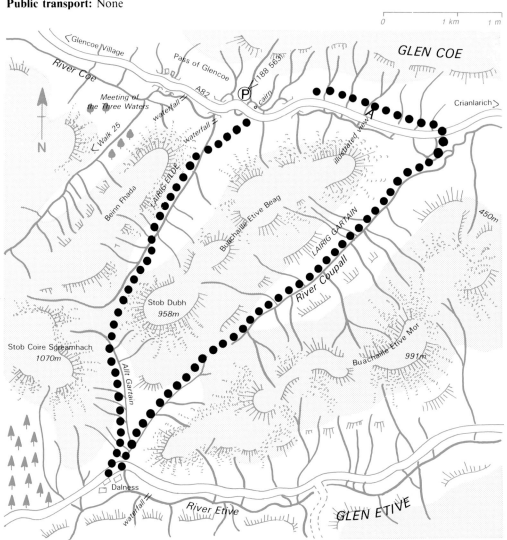

Walk 24

There are few places in the Highlands more famous than Glen Coe, and fewer still which can match its harsh grandeur. Here the moulding and carving of fire and ice, volcano and glacier, have created a landscape of rugged hills, rising steeply into contorted knots of peaks and ridges, intersected by knife-crease glens and wide corries.

The glen proper runs 7½ miles from Glencoe village by Loch Leven, east to the headwaters of the River Coe on Buachaille Etive Beag *(the Little Herdsman of Etive)*. However, the term is usually extended to include the glen of the River Coupall, which runs south-east from Lairig Gartain, doubles around the eastern end of Buachaille Etive Mór and joins the River Etive, flowing south-west to Loch Etive.

The northern side of the glen is a single, steep curtain of hills, Aonach Eagach *(notched ridge),* permitting no northward tracks between Loch Leven and the Devil's Staircase *(23)*. The southern side is a more complex mass of hills. To the west the glens between the peaks run blindly into high corries, but to the east there are two narrow passes through to Glen Etive: Lairig Eilde and Lairig Gartain.

To reach this route, park to the east of the Pass of Glencoe: a narrow section of the glen where the A82 runs through a rocky defile and passes close to the waterfall at the Meeting of the Three Waters. There are parking places by the road side.

Start walking from a large cairn, beside which there is a sign indicating the route to Glen Etive. The rough path climbs a slight, heathery incline before entering the narrow, rocky lairig, between the low ridges of Buachaille Etive Beag and Beinn Fhada.

After 2 miles of gentle climbing the path reaches the watershed, with the rocky peak of Stob Coire Sgreamhach behind a high, wide corrie to the west.

Drop down, by the burn, to Dalness in Glen Etive. By tradition, this is where Derdriu and Noisu, the doomed lovers of the Ulster Cycle of tales, fled when they were hounded from Ireland by the pursuit of King Conchobor. In later years it was part of the land of the MacDonalds of Glen Coe, though its inhabitants avoided the initial onslaught of the Massacre of Glencoe, in 1692.

At Dalness the two lairigs meet. Cut back north-eastwards, into Lairig Gartain. The path is very steep and quickly disappears, but the way is clear enough: up the grassy slope by the burn side. From the watershed at the top of the burn there is a fine view down Glen Etive - a wider, less dramatic glen than Glen Coe - to Loch Etive *(27)*.

The ground is very wet on the watershed, and the going remains damp right along the path, which drops gently down the lairig by the side of the River Coupall. The path is faint and, after exiting the pass, it disappears completely. Simply choose a route through the thick heather moorland to the A82.

Cross the road and climb a short way up the slope opposite to join a track which runs along the glen, back towards the start of the walk.

1. *Buachaille Etive Mór (903m)* 2. *Stob na Doire (1011m)* 3. *Stob na Bròige (955m)* 4. *Lairig Gartain* 5. *Stob Coire* 6. *Buachaille Etive Beag* 7. *Lairig Eilde* 8. *Beinn Fhada (811m)* 9. *Gearr Aonach (691m)* 10. *Aonach Dubh* 11. *Meall Mór* 12. *Sgorr nam Fiannaidh*

25 Coire Gabhail

Length: 2½ miles (4km) or over, there and back
Height climbed: 650ft (200m)
Grade: B
Public conveniences: None
Public transport: None

A short, rough, steep, lineal track through breath-taking scenery; leading through a narrow glen to an upper valley surrounded by peaks.

'Coire Gabhail' approximately translates as 'Corrie of the Spoil', which gives a clue to the history of the glen. This was the hiding place of the MacDonalds of Glen Coe; where they stashed stolen cattle, or hid their own when it was under threat. This little glen, high amongst the southern peaks and easily defended, must have been useful to the clan on many occasions during its stormy history. For the walker it provides a relatively easy track, high into the heart of the dramatic hill country.

There are a number of parking places beside the A82 through Glen Coe. For this walk park just to the west of the waterfall by the road at the Meeting of the Three Waters.

Walk down towards the river and join the path running parallel to the road up the glen. Turn left along this, and then right, down to the river, which flows through a shallow, wooded glen at this point. Follow a flight of steps down to the river and cross a wooden bridge.

Beyond the river the path rises slowly over marshy ground before leading up into the rocky glen below the valley. The going is rough here; both the path and the burn running over large boulders which have fallen into the narrow, wooded glen from the cliffs on either side. Nonetheless, it is an enchanting place; full of clear, small waterfalls.

At the top of this glen the path climbs up over a rise, to the left of the burn, and a view of the corrie opens up: a small, flat area of grass and gravel, flanked by the rocky slopes of Gearr Aonach and Beinn Fhada, and cut to the south by the ridge of Bidean nam Bian and the conical peak of Stob Coire Sgreamhach.

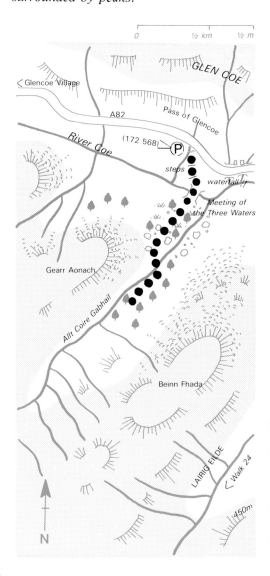

Walk 25

26 Glen Creran to Ballachulish

Length: 7 miles (11km) one way
Height climbed: 1200ft (370m) either way
Grade: A
Public conveniences: Ballachulish
Public transport: Ballachulish on bus route between Oban and Fort William

A steep hill climb, partly through thick forestry. Excellent mountain scenery. Possible alternative route to Duror.

To reach Glen Creran from Oban, drive 5 miles north, on the A85, to the Connel Bridge, and turn onto the A828 road towards Fort William. Just beyond the bridge at the head of Loch Creran a minor road cuts to the right. Follow this to its conclusion at Elleric car park.

From the car park there are two tracks. Take the left-hand track (the right-hand leads up Glen Ure: the home of Colin Campbell, the victim of the Appin Murder in 1746).

The track starts through mixed woodland, which quickly gives way to dense conifer forestry. After 1½ miles the track splits. Take the left-hand route, which climbs steeply, up into the high hills around the head of Glen Creran. Note the pieces of slate in the soil along the track. The seams of high-quality slate through these hills were profitably quarried at Ballachulish from as early as 1761, and the extraction continued until recent times.

1½ miles beyond the split the main track ends and an older, rougher track continues climbing steeply through the forest; finally breaking out of the trees on the narrow col between Fraochaidh and Sgorr a'Choise. From the col there are splendid views of the surrounding peaks; notably the scree slopes of Beinn a'Bheithir, directly ahead.

Climb over the stile on the col and follow the small glen beyond, down towards Gleann an Fhiodh. There is no clear path in the upper part of the glen; aim to cross to a cairn on the hill opposite. From this cairn one path cuts upstream, before Beinn a'Bheithir, leading 5½ miles to Duror. Downstream the path leads to Ballachulish village by Loch Leven.

27 Loch Etive

Length: Any distance, up to 11 miles
(17.5km) to Bonawe (one way)
Height climbed: Negligible
Grade: A/B
Public conveniences: None
Public transport: None

*A rough, damp lineal path running by
the side of a long sea-loch. Moorland,
conifers and broad-leaved woodland
along the way.*

Loch Etive is a long, thin sea-loch; winding
some 18 miles from the churning, tidal Falls
of Lora under the Connel Bridge, at the
mouth of the loch, back into the high hills.
For most of its length the loch is inaccessible
except on foot. There are rough footpaths
along both sides of the loch.

To reach the head of Loch Etive, drive
to the eastern end of Glen Coe and turn off
the A82 around the eastern end of Buachaille
Etive Mór *(the Herdsman of Etive)*, down the
minor road signposted to the glen. It is some
13 miles down this single-track road to the
head of the loch.

Where the road ends there is an open
area for parking, by an old pier. Start
walking along a faint, rough and very wet
footpath which leads down the west side of
the loch. The cover at the upper end of the
loch is a mixture of open moorland and
patches of mixed woodland: birch, holly,
rowan, ash and oak.

The surrounding hills are composed
entirely of granite, and fall steeply on either
side of the upper loch. To the west is Beinn
Trilleachan, with its great water-washed slabs
set into the hillside, and to the east is Ben
Starav.

This path continues for 11 miles down to
Bonawe.

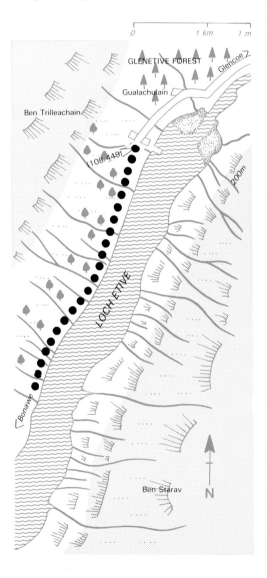

28 Bridge of Orchy to Inveroran

Length: 5½ miles (9km)
Height climbed: 550ft (170m) either way
Grade: B
Public conveniences: None
Public transport: Rail service from Fort
William; bus service from Oban.

*A short hill crossing, partly through
forestry, with fine views of the
surrounding hills. Back by public road
through a forest of Scots pine.*

Bridge of Orchy is a small village with a
hotel, just off the southern edge of Rannoch
Moor. This walk involves a short climb onto
Mam Carraigh, the ridge jutting into the gap
between Glen Orchy and Loch Tulla, from
which there are splendid views of the hills
around the moor.

Park at the village, on the A82 Fort
William to Glasgow road, and follow the
A8005 across the stone bridge over the River
Orchy. This bridge was built as part of the
military road (constructed in the mid-18th
century) which the hill section of this path
follows.

Just beyond the far end of the bridge
turn left, off the road, over a stile and into a
plantation of conifers. The path is clear but
wet, slanting up the side of the hill to the
upper edge of the plantation. At the edge of

the trees there is another stile, beyond which
the path climbs across grassy moorland to a
cairn at the top of the ridge. From the ridge
there are views west and north to the knot of
hills between Glen Etive and Rannoch Moor;
and east to Beinn Dòrain and the other peaks
beyond Glen Orchy.

The path drops down from the ridge to
Inveroran Hotel, near the head of Loch
Tulla. The West Highland Way (which also
follows this path) then continues northwards,
over the Black Mount towards Kingshouse
and Glen Coe.

To complete this route, cut right, along
the metalled road by Loch Tulla, back to
Bridge of Orchy. The road passes through an
area of Scots pine, birch and rowan. This is
one of the few remaining areas of naturally
sown pine woodland in Scotland.

29 Bridge of Orchy to Tyndrum

Length: 7 miles (11km) one way
Height climbed: 250ft (80m) walking south
Grade: B
Public conveniences: Tyndrum
Public transport: Bus and rail links from
Oban and Fort William.

*A long, lineal track along a broad
Highland glen, between two points linked
by the railway. Excellent hill scenery.*

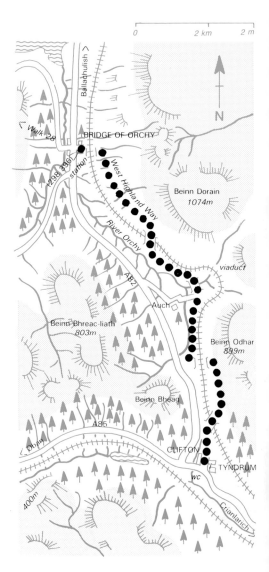

This route runs along the flanks of the hills
to the east of Glen Orchy, following the line
of the old military road, built in the mid-18th
century and now incorporated into the West
Highland Way. The A82 Glasgow to Fort
William road passes both ends of the route,
as does the West Highland railway line and,
since there are stations at both ends of the
route, one option is to take the train from
one village to the other and then walk back.

Bridge of Orchy is a small group of
cottages, a station and a hotel. Start walking
from the station. There is a tunnel under the
railway line, leading onto a rough track along
the hillside above it. The route is clear and
the walking comfortable, along the edge of a
broad U-shaped valley; eroded by a glacier
spilling south from Rannoch Moor during the
ice age. Along the valley floor the little river
meanders across the thin strip of flat land;
dwarfed by the great hills on either side. The
track runs along the side of Beinn Dòrain *(the
Hill of the Otter)*; a tall, neat, conical peak,
ribbed with lines of scree and small burns.
This mountain was celebrated in a famous
poem - 'Moladh Beinn Dòbhrain' *(In Praise
of Beinn Dòrain)* - by the 18th century Gaelic
poet Duncan Bán Macintyre.

At Auch the track cuts down across the
valley floor, while the railway loops eastward
to cross the Allt Kinglass by a great viaduct.
Beyond this the path rises again, through a
narrow pass, and then drops slowly towards
the joined villages of Clifton and Tyndrum.
Clifton was built in the 18th century to house
workers in the local lead mines; Tyndrum is a
busy stop-over for travellers along the A82.

30 Clach Thoull

Length: 1½ miles (2.5km)
Height climbed: Negligible
Grade: C
Public conveniences: Port Appin
Public transport: None

A short walk on clear paths, around the raised beach of a headland; backed by cliffs covered in mixed woodland.

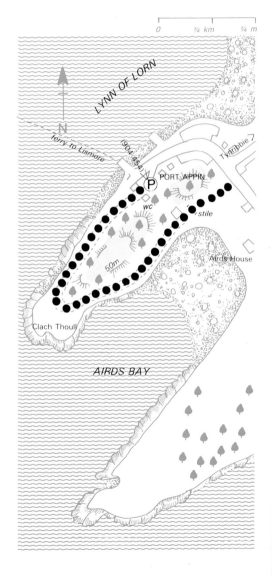

To reach Clach Thoull from Oban drive 5 miles north on the A85 to Connel Bridge; turn onto the A828 road to Fort William, across the bridge and around the head of Loch Creran, for 18 miles to the garage at Tynribbie. Turn left at the garage, onto the minor road to Port Appin. From the road there are excellent views of the 15th century Stewart stronghold of Castle Stalker, on a rock in the silted mouth of Loch Laich.

Port Appin is a pleasant little village, looking across the narrow Lynn of Lorn to the north end of the island of Lismore *(31)*, and to the mountains of Morvern beyond.

Follow the road down to the jetty (from which the passenger ferry crosses to Lismore) and park at the car park, where there is a sign indicating the 'Public Footpath to Clach Thoull'.

The path runs along a raised beach around the headland to the south of Port Appin. Behind this terrace there is a great block of quartzite, covered in a thick vegitation of rhododendrons, Scots pine, rowan, oak, larch, beech and others. Here and there - most dramatically upon the east side - the rock forms into great pale cliffs; marked with shallow caves amd fissures. At the southern end of the hill there is a tall arch, eroded out of the cliffs, from where there are splendid views of the islands of Lismore, Eriska (at the mouth of Loch Creran), Kerrera and Mull, and of the small islands scattered along the Lynn of Lorn.

Beyond the arch the path doubles back by the side of Airds Bay, at the head of which is the 18th century Airds House. At the path end turn left down a quiet public road to return to the car park.

31 Lismore

Length: Up to 10 miles (16km) plus extensions
Height climbed: 200ft (60m)
Grade: A/B/C
Public conveniences: Achnacroish; Port Appin
Public transport: None to Port Appin. Ferries
to Lismore from Port Appin and Oban.

*A series of quiet public roads and rough
tracks around this peaceful island.
Possible extensions along the way.*

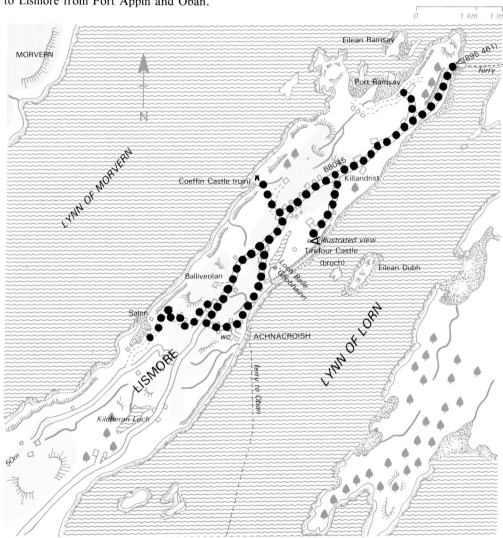

Lismore is one of the most delightful of Scotland's western islands. It is about 10 miles in length: long, thin low and green; lying at the junction of Loch Linnhe with the Sound of Mull and the Firth of Lorn, and surrounded by the mountains of Appin, Morvern and Mull.

The island is entirely rural - with the exception of small settlements at Achnacroish and Port Ramsay - and generally given over to sheep and cattle rearing. There is one shop at Balliveolan. The majority of the walking is on quiet public roads, but there are possible extensions along rough tracks.

Starting from the north end, which is reached by taking the small passenger ferry from Port Appin, the road runs along a raised beach (a feature of the coasts throughout this area). There is a cliff to the right of the road, covered in broad-leaved woodland and fuchsias. The growth is generally vigorous throughout the island; partly because of its mild climate, and partly because it is formed almost entirely of Limestone. This fertility is possibly at the root of the island's name - 'Lios Mór': the great garden. The strata of the island's limestone has been tilted on edge, forming a peculiar landscape: long, fertile strips running lengthwise down the island, separated by low, angular, broken ridges of rock.

The first road to the right cuts down to the little row of cottages at Port Ramsay,

sitting by a shallow, rock-strewn bay. The first to the left heads to the ruined broch at Tirefour. The remaining masonry stands on a low hill, above the cliffs overlooking the Lynn of Lorn (see illustration).

A little under a mile beyond the turn to Tirefour is the parish church, up to the right of the road. This building is partly constructed of the remains of a small cathedral; built in the 13th-14th centuries. Lismore has a long religious association; dating from the 6th century, when Columba (so the story goes) wished to use the island (which was ideally situated at the cross-roads of the major glens) as a base for his community, but was beaten in a race to the island by Moluag, who founded his own church here. In later years, when the cathedral was standing, the Bishops of Argyll stayed at Achadun Castle, at the southern end of the island. Following the Reformation the cathedral quickly fell into ruin.

A rough track, cutting off the road a short distance after the church, leads to the ruins of another castle, Coeffin, on a steep mound above a little bay. This was a viking stronghold, built in the 13th century.

Another point of interest is the deserted settlement at Salen. Salen, like Port Ramsay, was built to house quarrymen, who worked the limestone cliffs behind the houses. The last of the lime boats left the shallow harbour in the early part of this century.

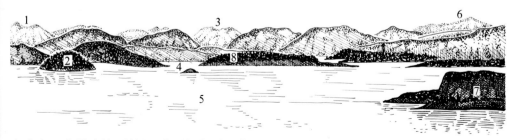

1. *Beinn a' Bheithir (1024m)* 2. *Clach Thoull* 3. *Beinn Sgulaird (937m)* 4. *Loch Creran*
5. *Lynn of Lorn* 6. *Ben Cruachan (1126m)* 7. *Eilean Dubh* 8. *Eriska*

32 Beinn Lora

Length: 3 miles (5km) there and back
Height climbed: 1000ft (300m)
Grade: B
Public conveniences: None
Public transport: Bus service between Oban and Fort William passes Benderloch

A steep forest walk, leading onto open moorland, and up to a summit. Splendid views of mountains and coastal scenery.

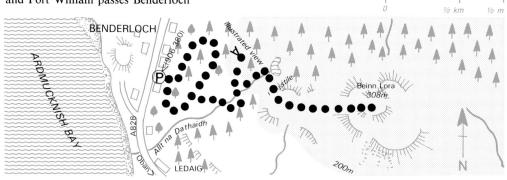

Beinn Lora sits above a junction of the major lochs and sounds of the area; providing views in all directions. South, across the mouth of Loch Etive, and down the Firth of Lorn to Kerrera and the islands beyond; west to Lismore, in the middle of Loch Linnhe, and beyond to the mountains of Morvern and Mull; and north to upper Loch Linnhe, Loch Creran and mountains of Appin. This is one of the finest viewpoints in the area, and not too difficult to reach.

The little village of Benderloch sits by Ardmucknish Bay, 2 miles north of the Connel Bridge on the road from Oban to Fort William. At the southern end of the village there is a small car park, and a path leads into the trees on the steep slope behind. The cover is predominantly coniferous, with occasional stands of broad-leaved trees. The paths are good on this lower stretch.

There are a number of paths leading to viewpoints within the forest. To reach Beinn Lora, turn up beside the burn, past a reedy lochan and on to a stile at the edge of the forest. From the stile the peak is clear: ½ mile out across the open hill.

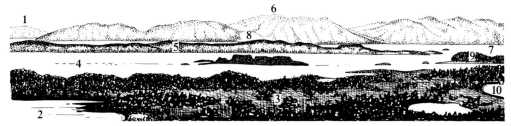

1. *Mull* 2. *Ardmucknish Bay* 3. *Benderloch* 4. *Lynn of Lorn* 5. *Lismore* 6. *Morvern*
7. *Loch Linnhe* 8. *Glensanda Quarry* 9. *Clach Thoull* 10. *Loch Creran*

33 Oban to Connel

Length: 5 miles (8km) one way
Height climbed: 250ft (80m)
Grade: B
Public conveniences: Oban
Public transport: Bus services to Oban from all directions; and linking Oban and Connel.

A clear, rough track merging with a public road; passing through quiet farmland. Possible return route on quiet public road.

Connel sits on the southern shore of Loch Etive, where the loch narrows as it nears its junction with the Firth of Lorn. When the tide is running strongly the water rushes through the narrows at great speed and with considerable turbulence. To avoid the ferry trip across this dangerous stretch of water (and to carry the now disused Oban to Fort William railway line) the Connel Bridge was built in 1903. It is a dramatic structure, not unlike a miniature Forth Rail Bridge.

This walk starts at the west end of Connel. Walk out along the A85 towards Oban. The road runs along the side of the loch at this point, giving views back up to the bridge. As it leaves the town the road rises and, near the top of a low hill, a track cuts from it, off to the left. Follow the track, through grazing land and past a stand of conifers.

The route is very simple from this point; the walking easy and the track clear. After a short distance it comes up to run parallel with the Oban-Glasgow railway line. On the bank of the line there is mixed woodland, while stretching away to the right there is a broad, shallow glen of hilly farmland.

The track gradually rises for 1½ miles before merging into a metalled road and slowly dropping down towards Oban. After 1 mile the road reaches a junction. Keep to the right at this point and continue down Glen Cruitten Road towards the centre of the town.

The two towns are linked by bus and rail. Also, there is a minor road to the east of the railway line which provides an alternative return route.

34 Ben Cruachan

Length: 7 miles (11km)
Height climbed: 3550ft (1070m)
Grade: A
Public conveniences: None
Public transport: Bus and rail services from Oban

A steep hill climb up one of the most impressive peaks in the area. The views are wonderful, but the going is very rough in places.

Ben Cruachan (3693ft/1126m) rises in a cluster of seven peaks to the north of Loch Awe, and from the highest summit there are wonderful views in all directions – notably westwards, across Loch Linnhe to the hills of Morvern and Mull. The hill is best known for supplying the Campbells with their war cry, and for the hydro-electric power station at its foot, with its underground turbines. This latter provides a useful pointer for the start of the route. To reach the walk, drive eastwards from Oban along the A85. After 12 miles the road passes through Taynuilt and shortly afterwards enters the narrow Pass of Brander, with an arm of Loch Awe to the right of the road. Watch for the entrance to the power station and park in one of the large lay-bys to the left of the road shortly beyond.

To start the walk, look for the sign for a footpath leading to the railway line. Follow this path uphill for a short distance, but when it turns left carry straight on, through a gate, under the railway line, and on along a rough, steep path which winds through broad-leaved woodland up the eastern side of a narrow glen.

After leaving the trees, watch for the point where the path crosses the burn, shortly before reaching a tarmac road. Turn left along this road and follow it up to the foot of the dam, visible ahead. Turn left again and climb up to join the clear track which runs from the end of the dam up the western side of the reservoir.

Follow this track to its conclusion then turn left on a rough path up a narrow glen. This leads up to the col between the peaks of Meall Cuanail and Ben Cruachan. Turn right from the col and scramble up the loose rocks to the summit of the hill.

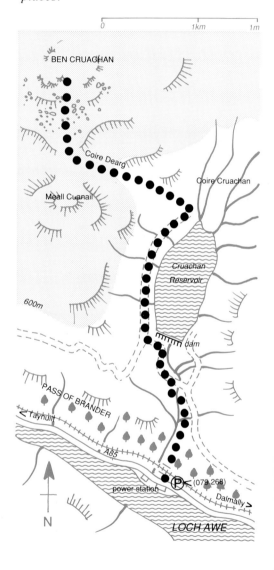

35 Oban to Gallanach

Length: Up to 5½ miles (9km)
Height climbed: 200ft (60m)
Grade: B
Public conveniences: Oban
Public transport: Bus services to Oban from all directions; rail service from the south.

Out on a short, rough hill track; back by quiet public roads. Extensive views of islands and headlands in the Firth of Lorn.

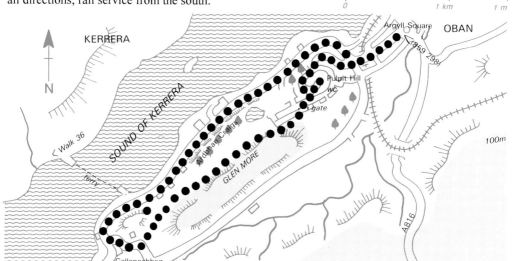

Start this walk from Argyll Square in Oban and follow the road signposted for Gallanach. After a short distance cut left up the road signposted for 'Pulpit Hill'.

The road cuts up through the trees and houses which cling to the face of the steep hill, and then circles round behind it, before doubling back and re-emerging on a clear patch of land facing north, at the top of the hill. From here there are excellent views of Oban and Oban Bay, and over Loch Linnhe to Morvern and Mull.

Double back from this point and take the first road to the left. Almost immediately there is another choice. This time go right. A short way along this road there is a gate to the left. Go through this and follow the path beyond, along behind the houses.

The buildings are soon left behind, and the clear track continues through grazing land between two low ridges. **Please be careful to avoid disturbing farm animals along this stretch of the route.**

After about 1 mile the track splits. The left-hand track climbs up, through a low pass, and then drops down to the public road south of Gallanachbeg. The right-hand track shortens the route; cutting straight down to the coast and joining the road by the jetty for the Kerrera ferry *(36)*.

Either way, follow the road north, under the shadow of the steep, wooded Ardbhan Craigs – along the edge of the Sound of Kerrera to Oban. This is a lovely road, with views across the anchorage by the sailing club. However, the road is walled and very narrow, so listen carefully for approaching cars and keep in to the side.

36 Kerrera

Length: 7 miles (11km)
Height climbed: 350ft (100m)
Grade: B
Public conveniences: None
Public transport: Ferry from Gallanach

A sequence of tracks and paths around a quiet island. Splendid views of the Firth of Lorn. Route passes ruined Gylen Castle.

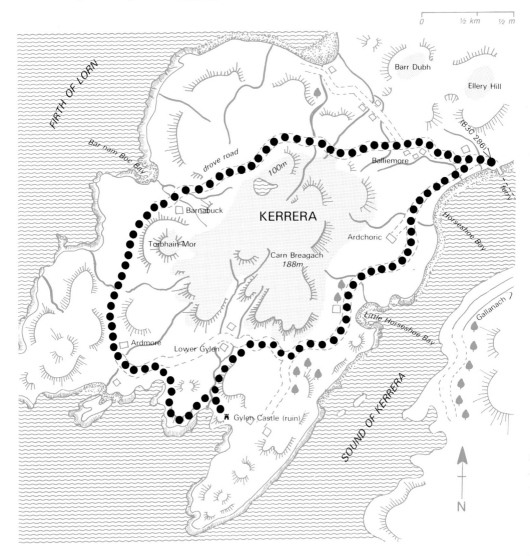

Kerrera is a small island (4 miles long and 2 miles wide at its broadest point) in the Firth of Lorn. Along its eastern side it is less than ½ mile off shore; seperated from the mainland by the narrow Sound of Kerrera. At the northern end of the sound it swells into the bulb of Oban Bay before narrowing again to the north. Kerrera thus forms the harbour-wall which has enabled Oban to develop as a fishing port and ferry terminus.

The island is generally green, but very rocky and undulating. At its highest point, Carn Breagach, it is a little over 600ft in height. It is fringed by raised beaches which provide a certain amount of flat land. The island is entirely given over to small farms, with one boatyard on Oban Bay at its northern tip.

There are a number of paths around the island; this route involves a circuit of its southern end. The paths are a little faint in places, but it is difficult to go far wrong in so confined a space.

To reach Kerrera drive south from Oban on the minor coast road, signposted to Gallanach. The jetty for the ferry is about 2 miles from the centre of Oban. It may be necessary to signal for the ferry if it is on the Kerrera side.

Once on the island follow the track up from the jetty and cut left, along the track by the coast.

Until 1266 Kerrera, along with all the other islands off Scotland's northern and western coasts, belonged to Norway. Horseshoe Bay, to the south of the jetty, was twice the scene of important acts in the disputes of ownership between the Norse and Scottish kings. In 1249 Alexander II, King of Scotland, died here when leading an army against the Hebrides; and, in 1263, King Haakon of Norway gathered a fleet of ships from the islands in the bay. His force was defeated by the Scots, under Alexander III, at the Battle of Largs; a defeat which virtually ensured Scottish sovereignty over the Western isles.

Since the days when the islands belonged to Norway Kerrera has been the property of the MacDougalls, whose main stronghold was at Dunollie, north of Oban.

Follow the track along the coast, cutting inland south of Little Horseshoe Bay. Cut off this track a little before Lower Gylen and follow a rough path down to Gylen Castle.

Gylen was built at the end of the 16th century by Duncan MacDougall of Dunollie, the 16th chief. It is a rare example (for the west coast) of a tower built in the Scots Baronial style: tall, thin and L-shaped. It is much smaller than the examples to the east of the Grampians, but it matches them for its exquisite proportions, and its position is better than any: perched above a cliff between two narrow inlets. Sadly, the castle was besieged, taken and burnt by the Covenanters in 1647 and, although occasional repairs to the masonry have kept the walls intact, Gylen has never been rebuilt.

Continue along the coast until the track is regained, and follow this to Ardmore. Pass to the left of the farm and follow a rough path through a narrow gap and then down, around the foot of a steep slope, to the farmhouse at Barnabuck.

Cut up from the shore, climbing up a broad track into the heathery interior of the island. This track was once a link in the drove road from the islands to the west - Mull, Coll, Tiree - to the great cattle fairs, or trysts, in the south. Every year, until the mid 19th century, 2000 cattle or more would be shipped from Grass Point, on the south side of Loch Don on Mull, to Kerrera. They would be driven across the island and would then swim across the narrow channel to the mainland.

Follow the track over the centre of the island, admiring the fine views across the Firth of Lorn, and then drop back down to the ferry.

Walk 36

37 Glen Nant

Length: 2½ miles (4km)
Height climbed: 250ft (70m)
Grade: C
Public conveniences: None
Public transport: Bus service from Oban

A short, signposted walk through semi-natural oak woodland. Paths good. Good view of Ben Cruachan.

To reach this walk, first find Taynuilt - 12 miles east of Oban on the A85 - and then turn onto the B845. 2 miles along this road there is a car park, across a bridge to the right of the road. Pass through the gate out of the car park and follow the signs through the wood.

This part of Glen Nant is clothed in mixed broad-leaved woodland, predominantly oak. Ironically, its survival was due largely to the building of the Bonawe Iron Furnace at Taynuilt in 1753. A steady supply of charcoal was required for the furnace, and this was produced by controlled burning of the local hardwoods. The woodland was managed to keep local supplies high.

Along this route there are displays describing the techniques employed by the charcoal burners; including a mock-up of one of their fires; covered with turfs to ensure that the wood burnt slowly. In addition there are descriptions of the wildlife which may be found here. The oakwoods are particularly rich in insect life; including large colonies of wood ants, whose nests can reach 4ft in height. Ground cover tends to be of mosses, lichens, bracken and grasses. Also, throughout this wood, there are a great many birch trees. Plants include wood anemone, primrose, cow wheat, orchids, blaeberry and bluebell. Roe deer may be seen.

There are views from the northern end of the walk up Glen Nant, and also east, across the Pass of Brander to the peaks of Ben Cruachan.

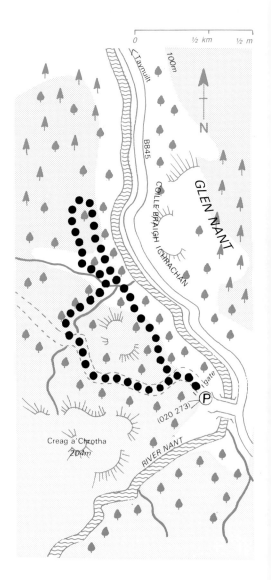

38 Dalavich Oakwood

Length: 1½ miles (2.5km)
Height climbed: 150ft (40m)
Grade: C
Public conveniences: None
Public transport: Bus service from Oban

A short, signposted track through an area of oakwood. Paths generally good.

To reach Dalavich from Oban, leave the town on the A85. Follow the road for 12 miles, past the village of Taynuilt. A little beyond the village, just over the bridge across the River Nant, the B845 cuts off to the right. Follow this road to Kilchrenan and then follow the signs for Dalavich. The car park for this route is at Barnaline, a little before Dalavich, by the River Avich.

As at Glen Nant *(37)* and Ariundle *(6)*, this walk is through semi-natural oakwood, intermixed with birch, ash, rowan and others, managed during the 18th and 19th centuries to provide charcoal for the Bonawe Iron Furnace at Taynuilt. A section of the wood has been declared a Site of Special Scientific Interest and has been fenced off, to keep grazing animals out of the woods. The importance of the oakwoods is that they provide a suitable habitat for a great many more wild creatures and plants than do thick conifer plantations or open moorland.

The route is clearly signposted, and a leaflet is available locally explaining the history and management of the wood in greater detail.

Also starting from the car park at Barnaline is a short track around Avich Falls. Follow the forestry road out of the car park, cutting off it to the right, after a short distance, along a rough footpath which leads up through the wooded glen of the River Avich to a footbridge. Cross this and turn right onto a forest track. Follow the track down to a quiet public road and turn right. Turn right again at the next junction to return to the car park.

39 Timber Trail

Length: 2 miles (3km)
Height climbed: 200ft (60m)
Grade: C
Public conveniences: None
Public transport: None

A short forest walk, largely through conifers, along the edge of a large inland loch. Paths clear, but damp in places.

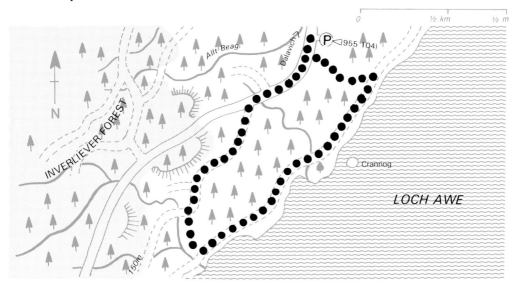

To reach the Timber Trail from Oban, leave the town on the A85, and continue on this road for 12 miles to Taynuilt. Just beyond the village, after the bridge over the River Nant, the B845 cuts off to the right. Follow this road to Kilchrenan, and then cut right on the minor road signposted to Dalavich. 2 miles beyond Dalavich, amongst the trees of Inverliever Forest, there is a small car park to the left of the road; just opposite a reedy field at a break in the forest.

Walk a short way south along the road and then cut left, down a signposted path, through a thick conifer plantation, interspersed with broad-leaved trees. The path is rough, but the route is clear enough.

After a short distance this path joins a track along the edge of Loch Awe, with a wood of mixed broad-leaved trees between the track and the water.

A short way along this track there is a sign pointing down to the water, leading to a view of an old crannog island: a low mound of rubble, covered in scrub, just offshore.

There are a number of these small islands in Loch Awe, which were made about two thousand years ago, and used as foundations for defensive houses. A round, wooden hut, surrounded by a platform balanced over the water on piles, would be built on the island, and joined to the mainland by a narrow bridge.

Continue along the main track until it enters a mixed stand of older tress - larch, beech, Douglas fir, Sitka spruce - around a small burn. Cut right, before the burn, and follow a rough path up through the plantation, to join a wider track. Cut right along this to return to the road.

40 Armaddy to Degnish

Length: 3½ miles (5.5km) one way
Height climbed: 400ft (120m)
Grade: B
Public conveniences: None
Public transport: None

A short hill crossing on clear paths of varying quality. Fine views of coastal scenery.

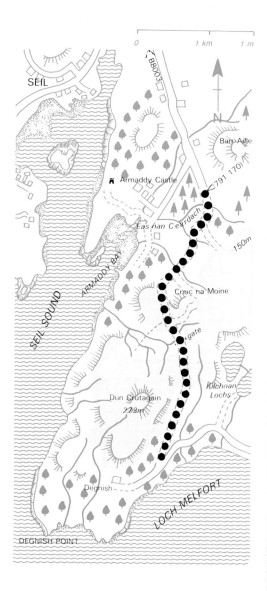

To reach this walk drive south from Oban for some 8 miles on the A816 road to Campbeltown. Turn right onto the B844 to Easdale; and then left onto a minor road to Armaddy. At the point where this road ends turn up the track to the left and park on the verge.

Start walking up the track beyond, which runs, at first, by the side of a conifer plantation and then, after crossing Eas Nan Ceardach *(Burn of the Smithies),* cuts along the open hillside.

The landscape is lumpy, with edges of rock jutting through a thin cover of grass and bracken. There are views westwards, across Armaddy Bay to the island of Seil.

The path cuts left and starts to climb steeply, towards a pass. A little before the throat of the pass there is an old hawthorn tree by the track-side, with hundreds of coins beaten into its bark. This practice is thought to bring luck.

Beyond the pass the track swings round to the left. There are two tracks cutting off to the right. Ignore the first (which is very faint) and take the second. This leads on across the high pastures to a ditch and a dyke with a gate in it. At this point the grassland ends and heather moorland takes over; dotted with bog asphodel, bog cotton and reeds.

The path gently rises and then drops down towards the wooded shore of Loch Melfort. Beyond the high point of the path there are splendid views south, to the islands of Shuna and Luing and the Craignish Peninsula.

The path ends at a minor public road; just by the gate to Degnish. Return by the same route.

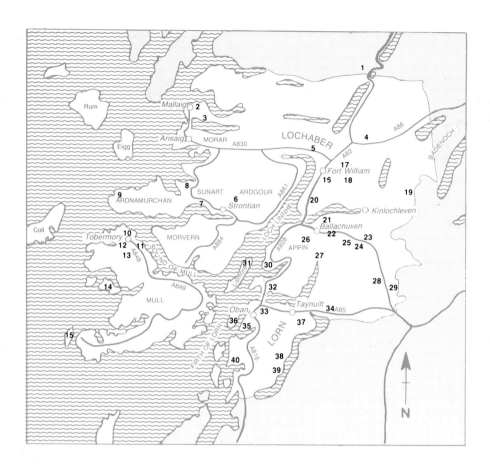

1
Mallaig 2
3
Rum
Arisaig MORAR A830 LOCHABER
Eigg 4 A86
5 A82
17 Fort William
15 18 BADENOCH
8 SUNART ARDGOUR
9 6 19
Coll ARDNAMURCHAN Strontian 20
7 A861 LOCH LINNHE
21
10 Tobermory MORVERN Ballachulish Kinlochleven
12 11 A884 22 23
13 A848 26 25 24
SOUND OF MULL A828 APPIN 27
31 30 28 29
14 A849 32
MULL Oban Taynuilt 34 A85
36 33 37
15 35 LORN
FIRTH OF LORN 40 A816 38
39

N